Story
Sparks

Also by Denise Jaden

FICTION

Avalanche

A Christmas Kerril

Foreign Exchange

Losing Faith

Never Enough

BOOKS FOR WRITERS

Fast Fiction

Writing with a Heavy Heart

Story
Sparks

Finding Your Best Story Ideas
& Turning Them into
Compelling Fiction

DENISE JADEN

New World Library
Novato, California

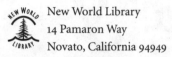

New World Library
14 Pamaron Way
Novato, California 94949

Text design by Tona Pearce Myers

Library of Congress Cataloging-in-Publication data is available.

First printing, August 2017
ISBN 978-1-60868-509-7
Ebook ISBN 978-1-60868-510-3
Printed in Canada on 100% postconsumer-waste recycled paper

New World Library is proud to be a Gold Certified Environmentally Responsible Publisher. Publisher certification awarded by Green Press Initiative. www.greenpressinitiative.org

10   9   8   7   6   5   4   3   2   1

To all the writers who have ever wondered
whether their ideas are good enough

Contents

Introduction

One of the most common questions I'm asked when I speak to groups of writers is "Where do you get your story ideas?" No matter which of my books we are talking about, I always have a story behind the story. Not only that, but I can usually remember the spark that nestled itself into my heart and burned strong and bright enough to carry me through hundreds of pages of writing.

I know that sounds easy, and I can already sense what you're probably thinking: *It must be nice to have awesome fully formed ideas right from the onset and then simply sit down to transcribe them.* No, that's not how it works, at least not for me. At the beginning, the nature of the spark is often obscure. However, by the end, and after much revision and digging to find the heart of that story, I can look back and see an illuminated spark at the center of it, like, "Oh, right, *that's* what drove me!"

This book is broken into five parts. Part 1 delves into S.P.A.R.K., which is my acronym for the way story ideas work and why they resonate with us. Part 2 is an encyclopedia of methods for stirring up more ideas. Part 3 offers instruction into following through on story development. Part 4 is a practical guide for establishing story-forming habits. And the appendixes constitute the book's fifth part. These are idea factories or cheat sheets you can turn to whenever you're stuck.

Speaking of being stuck, why do some writers seem to have endless character, story, and plotting ideas while others struggle? Is this a talent some writers are born with? If you've ever felt discouraged by this unbalance in the creative world, not to worry. Idea gathering is a highly learnable skill!

Ideas do not usually come to us already fully formed. In fact, some of my best story ideas first arrived as niggling and annoying insect-like thoughts that I originally suspected had little substance and were only there to distract me. Don't be afraid of tiny ideas or half-formed ideas. Have faith. If ideas are meant to create stories, given time and focus they *will* grow and complete themselves. When you're writing and you don't have all the answers, learn to leave plenty of blank spaces and keep moving. Create forward momentum for yourself and your stories. Even while writing this book, I left plenty of blank spaces along the way and came back to flesh them out later.

One of the main goals of this book is to ensure that a lack of ideas doesn't stop you up in your writing. Later, I discuss writer's block, which is not usually a lack of ideas. It's a lack of what you consider *worthy* ideas, and the solution is frequently to keep moving forward using any and all ideas, even bad ideas, so that you're not stuck staring at a blank page. In my previous book about writing, *Fast Fiction*, my solution for perfectionism is to write forward, write lots, write badly, and basically just keep writing. It's the same with ideas: just keep finding, developing, merging, and combining ideas until your story is moving.

Allowing your ideas to spark and grow takes planning and forming good habits. It means understanding that ideas matter. Creativity is the structure of our existence. Maybe the general population doesn't notice how much ideas matter, but talk to teachers, inventors, managers, advertisers, business owners, authors.... They all rely on and cultivate precious and important new ideas every single day. What do cars and airplanes and buildings and toothpaste and fashion and the internet and cell phones and *Moby Dick* all have in common? They were all sparked by ideas. Our society and human existence, everything we do and use, reflects our creativity.

This book's aim is to equip you with skills and methods to uncover *your* best ideas and grow them to fruition. To kick-start this process, I'd like to ask you a few questions:

What kind of writer are you? Fast? Slow? A thorough outliner? A write-by-the-seat-of-your-pantser? How have you come up with your story ideas so far? Does this method change for each story you write?

What kinds of stories do you want to tell? Genre fiction or contemporary realism? What kinds of stories do you like to read? What kinds of stories excite you most? What are the best endings you've ever read? The best beginnings? What stirs you up? What bores you to tears?

Before turning the page, spend a few minutes thinking about your answers to these questions. No matter what your answers, you're not wrong! Everyone's brainstorming process is different, and creative people often brainstorm differently from project to project. How do you typically brainstorm story ideas? Does a particular kind of story beckon you to write it? Do you gravitate toward simple linear stories or complex, multi-timeline, multi-point-of-view kaleidoscopes? Your answers to these questions can help guide your brainstorming, as this book takes you on a personal journey to spark the stories only you can tell.

Go ahead, turn the page. Strike the match.

Part I

S.P.A.R.K.

From a little spark may burst a mighty flame.
— **DANTE ALIGHIERI**

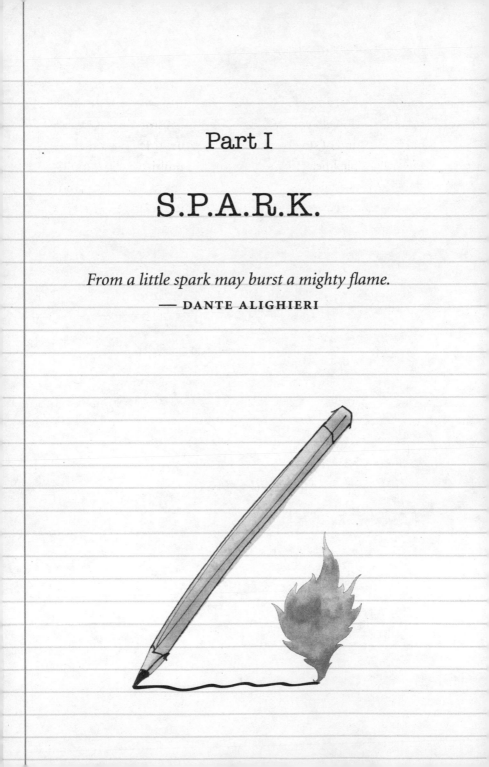

Great ideas can spark like a fire — once they catch, they can burst fast and furiously into full heat in a matter of seconds. Or, ideas can grow like a garden — slow and consistent, sprouts breaking ground, plants rising and standing on their own, and bringing forth fruit in the proper season with plenty of watering and sunshine. Sometimes ideas can steep like a cup of tea — as you stir them, you can actually see the ideas getting stronger, deeper, and more pungent.

Ideas can even come into our lives like drunks, flailing along on the sides of the road, shouting and confused, and no good to anyone until you help sober them up. Have you ever heard of a "pizza dream" — the idea that having too much junk food and pizza causes the craziest dreams?

The truth is, ideas appear in our lives in all sorts of ways and rarely in the same way twice. This is what makes it tough to find a method of locating and harnessing them. But the more we understand about how ideas are formed and how they expand, the more we will cultivate abundance in our creative lives.

I came up with the acronym S.P.A.R.K. to help capture the anatomy of story idea development. S.P.A.R.K. stands for seek, passion, allies, resonance, and kinetic energy.

1. Seek

*We live in a wonderful world that is full of beauty,
charm, and adventure. There is no end to the adventures
that we can have if only we seek them with our eyes open.*

— JAWAHARLAL NEHRU

Why does the symbol of a lightbulb indicate a new idea? The word *idea* is from the Greek word "idiom," which means "to see."

Everybody needs ideas. Advertisers, inventors, PTA members, hockey moms, personal trainers, restaurant owners. In this information age, computers can now take care of a great deal of administrative work. Programs and apps can help you develop an outline or synopsis. Grammar software can help you choose wording and assist in sentence construction. What is, and what will always be, in shorter supply is the ability to come up with great story ideas in the first place.

This is easier than you think! A fresh idea is simply thinking of something in a new way or combining two concepts in a unique way. Robert Frost tells us, "If you remember only one thing I've said, remember that an idea is a feat of association."

Idea making is for everyone, not only for the especially in-genious. It's for the mom making soup with what she has left in the fridge, the contractor making a building more efficient, and the fourth-grade teacher seeking to reach all of her students.

As you probably know, the brain is divided into two hemi-spheres: The left side is the more cognitive, analytical side, while the right side is the more associative, creative side. This is true, but idea creation is more complicated than that. The superior temporal gyrus resides in both sides of your brain, and that's where flashes of insight occur. I think we can all agree, flashes of insight, those moments when your brain relaxes and comes up with a solution you'd never thought of before, are absolutely essential to the creative process!

But no matter how active and developed your superior tem-poral gyrus, ideas won't always simply come to you. You must become an Idea Seeker and seek them out.

Make a habit of looking for ideas. Don't wait to brainstorm until you've written yourself into a corner. Dr. Linus Pauling tells us, "If you want to have good ideas, you must have many ideas."

As an Idea Seeker, choose quantity over the quality of ideas. First, it's often difficult to recognize the quality of an idea when it arises. An idea may look humdrum until it's fed into the right story at the right time, or until it is combined with another idea to create the perfect solution.

Gathering a plethora of ideas does not necessarily take smarts or even creativity. It simply means diligently keeping your eyes open for new ideas or new connections between ideas. In fact, highly intelligent people often overestimate their smarts, and they value too highly a single idea that they focus on exclusively, while underestimating the power in simply observing.

Idea Seekers always actively search for new inspiration. Then, once they have gathered a sufficient number of ideas, this propels them to create with those ideas. Idea seeking and implementing is a cycle that feeds itself. By developing an almost insatiable appetite for acquiring and using new ideas, you will discover that the act of finding and using ideas continually sparks the creation of even more ideas.

But you don't become an Idea Seeker overnight. It takes time to discover what, specifically, sparks your creativity, joy, anger, and sorrow. Make notes of what you feel and what causes your reactions.

Seek inside yourself. What are you good at, or what do you think you might be good at? Be a fly on the wall to yourself and explore what piques your interest. What do you already know about, and what do you want to know about? For example, if you're interested in golf, consider *why* this interests you. Is it the focus the sport requires, or the particular skill of hitting a tiny ball a long range with accuracy? Or is it the camaraderie of playing with a group, or the sport's particular humor, pace, history, or debates? Explore those areas and note your reactions.

Explore your interests in places and peoples. If you could go anywhere, where would it be and why? Explore the finer details of these locations. What type of people intrigue you the most and why? What, specifically, do you find interesting or engaging? Study the way people are and the traits that interest you. Imagine what it might feel like to be another person. Interview people with your idea-seeking eyes open. Were people born with the attributes you find most interesting? Or has life shaped them that way?

What do you return to again and again? Is there a type of person or job or pastime you usually gravitate to? If you were going to reread five books, what would they be and why? What places do you enjoy visiting and what do they have in common? Take notice of what's already there. This is the starting point for finding new ideas.

What types of ideas are you most receptive to? Or, a better question might be, what ideas are you unreceptive to? Some folks arbitrarily reject popular ideas, while others gravitate to them. They feel safest with ideas and people who have already succeeded.

If I suggested that you write a story about a boy and his dog, what would your reaction be? Some ideas come to us and our inner voice shouts, "Yes!" while others barely extract a shoulder shrug. Explore why that is for you. If someone told you that an idea you consider boring would be the next bestseller, would you look at it differently? The value we place on ideas guides the ideas we choose to use in our stories. Rather than dismiss some ideas out of hand, treat all of your ideas as though, with a good shining, they could be gems. The fact that we are not receptive toward certain ideas usually says more about us than the quality of the ideas themselves.

I'm not saying you should embrace ideas that feel wrong. No. I'm only suggesting getting into the habit of considering every idea and, at the very least, filing it away. I'm suggesting breaking the habit of quickly rejecting certain ideas. Perhaps some ideas will never have emotional resonance with you, and that's okay! But some, given time, and combined with the right elements, could be the key you're looking for in order to complete a well-rounded plot. They could, eventually, take on a life of their own.

What about those ideas that do resonate with you? Which ideas leave you feeling sympathy or empathy for a person or a situation? Whittle down exactly what moves you. Knowing yourself will help you know your characters and what causes passionate reactions in your stories.

Think of your observational skills as muscles. The more you use them, the more they will develop, and the easier it will be to "lift weights" with barely any effort on your part, perhaps without even noticing.

Have you ever had an accidental idea? Think back to a time when you were trying to come up with a new plot idea for one story, and instead an idea from left field for a totally different story popped into your head. This is the great effect of relaxation helping you brainstorm. The part of your brain that is not über-focused on your first story is taking a walk through an airy park, feeling the wind through its brain tunnels, and this freedom is allowing ideas to rise up. Write them down! You don't have to take off on a tangent and fully plot out that new story right this second, but don't lose those ideas! Write down what comes to you easily. And when your brain moves on to something else and another accidental idea pops up about this new story, jot that down, too. Don't worry, you'll have plenty of time for that to become your "stress project" later! (And that's when you'll likely get fantastic new ideas for yet another story!)

Another thing to keep in mind is that sometimes what you

think you're looking for is not really what your story needs. Be open to anything, and allow your brainstorming mind some freedom. Your search may inadvertently lead you to what you really need in your story if you let yourself believe in the possibility. Even if your ideas seem to be going in a weird direction, write everything down and figure it out later.

Don't only look where everyone else is looking. Once you start looking for ideas without automatically discounting them, you'll start to find them everywhere.

Don't be afraid to dream wild and big, and don't be afraid of incomplete areas that still need to be developed and filled in. Don't let a lack of ideas stop you from writing. Simply leave blank spots in the story for now. Like a grade-school quiz, you can come back later and finish the tough questions after you've filled in the ones you know.

Put It into Practice

1. At your workplace, at school, or at any public place you frequent, have a meaningful conversation with three people you do not already know well. Learn at least three new things about each person, such as their dreams, most exciting experiences, and greatest fears. Ask about emotional reactions to events, secrets, habits, and quirks. Actively learn about people to discover material for fictional characters and plots.

2. Make a Spark List of new ideas that arise during your conversations or while out in public places. Describe the emotions these ideas spark and where the ideas might

take you if you followed them through. Ask questions and what-ifs about each scenario.

As an example, I've included a sample Spark List of my own for reference:

1. The grocery store clerk's name tag read "Chelsea" today. I stopped to ponder if she might have a nickname and what her friends would call her. "Chels," I decided. From there, I considered the smile she seemed to be suppressing. I pictured her meeting up with her friends after work, and wondered, "What's the coolest thing Chels could do after work today?" Is she single, but crushing on a guy in her friend group? Are they going to the fair, or hiking up a mountain, or trying bungee jumping for the first time? I thought back to the one time I considered bungee jumping, and along with a shot of fear, I felt an immediate respect and admiration for Chels.

2. At the gym, I noticed a scrawny guy who was giving the weights his all. At first, I was a little afraid he might hurt himself, but then my mind wandered to what would motivate him to work so hard in the gym. Does he get teased? Does he have a brother who's naturally beefy, and whom he's always been jealous of? Does he aspire to a well-paying job that involves heavy lifting? What would change for him if he put on ten pounds of muscle? Would he be more secure with himself, or would it still not be enough?

3. While on the elliptical machine at the gym, I watched an episode of a culinary competition show. One of the

chefs on the show bet all his "show dollars" on himself right at the onset of the show, while another was timid about using any of his "show dollars." It got me to thinking how different characters, and different people, deal with risk. Are some born being risk takers? Or does it have to do with family upbringing? Was the first chef just that much more confident in his ability? What if they were both taken out of the food realm, where they are experienced — would they bet the same way with real money in the stock market? Why does my heart rate skyrocket as I watch the stakes rise? How heavily would I bet on myself in, say, a writing competition, and would the adrenaline of betting on myself help or hinder my performance?

Now come up with your own Spark List. Where will life take you this week, and what about that journey interests you most?

2. Passion

Passion is one great force that unleashes creativity,
because if you're passionate about something,
then you're more willing to take risks.

— YO-YO MA

What do you love, connect to, or want to read when it comes to fiction? In this chapter, I'd like to delve into the heart of who you are and what you connect to most.

We've all heard the advice to "be yourself." But how well do you know yourself, and when it comes to creating other characters, what does that mean? We're also told to "follow your passion," but what if you don't know what, exactly, you're passionate about? I believe that everyone's *true self* has great stories that are full of life and just waiting to be told, but we have to seek and explore our true self to find those stories. We need passion to deliver us to the end of the process — where we find resonance and kinetic energy — but how on earth do you find it?

First, get rid of all the *shoulds* in your writing. What is your level of desire to write a new story or to finish the stories you are currently working on? Do you feel any sense of obligation about writing these stories? In her motivational book *Get It Done*, Sam Bennett suggests writing a "Could Do List." For instance, if you had unlimited time and resources, what might or could you do? Make this list, while understanding that you are under absolutely no obligation to follow through with any of these ideas. This is not a to-do list. It is a dream list that reveals what's inside you.

In your journal, answer the following questions: When do you feel most alive? When are you most in love? Most enraged? What motivates you? What wrecks you emotionally? What angers you most? Harness these feelings and memories to find new ideas, and use them to sift through your ideas once you have an overflowing abundance.

What is dangerous about your writing process? Do you anticipate and plan for readers of your work? Do you add plot obstacles or situations to your writing that feel risky, that feel like they may take your story in the wrong direction, or that feel beyond your ability as a writer to pull off? If you answer "nothing about my writing is dangerous," this may be a problem. If your writing feels humdrum, it may be because you don't have anyone waiting to read your stories, or your writing doesn't tackle high stakes. If you don't feel much while writing your stories, your readers may not feel a whole lot either.

What is your personality type? Are you an all-in kind of person or a hold-back type? Do you tend to look up to other personality types or automatically discredit them? What about yourself do you hold in highest regard? What about yourself do you wish you could change?

What are your most prized values? If you haven't, try writing a character with opposing values in a sympathetic way. Are you a dog lover? Write about a character who dislikes or is afraid of dogs. Are you always punctual? Try writing sympathetically about someone who is always running late. If your writing lacks vibrancy, try writing characters who conflict with you, and dig deep to discover their motivations. For your readers to feel deep emotions, you must write with deep emotion and passion.

As you discover new things about yourself and what inspires your passions, insert those ideas and motivations into your stories. At the end of the day, you want your stories to make readers feel as inspired as you felt when you first thought of them. Do your stories make you feel passionate? Do they inspire, invigorate, teach, and enlighten you? Have they helped you solve a problem? If you want them to do the same for your readers, they must.

The goal of knowing and recognizing the things that make you feel deeply is to inspire your writing, so I ask you this: Which ideas propel you to write?

Put It into Practice

1.   During a character-building workshop I teach, I tend to harp a lot on how the more we know ourselves, the more we will know our characters. That's why I start my character-building workshops with a personality quiz — not for the characters, but for the writers. (Later, I encourage students to complete the same quiz for their characters.) I like to use a fun and short online personality quiz from the Smalley Institute that features four

main personality types and names them after four animals: the lion, the otter, the golden retriever, and the beaver (see the endnotes for a link). But it doesn't matter which personality quiz you use. Others are more thorough or complicated, with more categories (and wanting one of these probably says something about your personality type!). Choose a personality quiz that interests you and fill it out today.

2. Once you've identified the strengths and weaknesses and relational propensities of your personality type, take a few minutes to write a mission statement for your writing and your life. By putting these ideas to paper, you define the purpose that guides all your writing. What is most important to you? What do you hope to focus on and bring across on the page? What do you hope to make readers feel?

This mission statement can be worded in any way you want, but consider writing it so that it answers questions like these:

1. What emotions do you want readers to feel most when they read your writing?
2. How do you envision improving or enriching your reader's life because of your writing?
3. Ideally, how do you want your writing to change the world in a meaningful way?
4. How does your writing benefit you? Is it cathartic? Does it enrich your understanding of the world? Does it add to your income?

I hope this section leads you to a greater understanding of your passions, and how these passions can fuel your writing. This is something we are always learning and discovering, since people are not static. We're ever-changing, for life changes us. So keep revisiting your passions and taking stock of how they are evolving over time.

3. Allies

I'm always glad when people come together to help each other —
whether they're raising money for somebody in a bad situation
or making a creative piece like a song.

— ZE FRANK

Writing is a solitary venture, but mining ideas is (or should be) a collaborative one. If you are relying solely on your own ideas in your storytelling, you may be missing out.

First, each of us sees the world through our own worldview, and everyone has their own. Why not work these different outlooks and ideas into your stories? Don't limit yourself to your own favorite names, places, and dreams, to your personal goals or the insurmountable obstacles you've faced. Widen the scope of your writing by drawing on the experiences, fears, and dreams of others.

Next, ideas grow by sharing them. If I have a car and you have a car, and we exchange them, we still each have one car. However, if I have an idea and you have an idea, and we exchange ideas, we will both have two ideas, which we can mate together to create even more ideas. Further, because people have different worldviews, they look at the same ideas differently, and they implement them very differently. There are no copyright laws on ideas, and thank goodness for that! How sad if no more war dramas could be written after *Saving Private Ryan*? Or if *Pride and Prejudice* was the last novel about love crossing societal classes?

Writers can be reluctant to share ideas for fear of overlap, but a quick scan of popular culture puts that to rest. Consider how many stories have been written about a struggling musician overcoming overwhelming odds to achieve his or her dream and become a superstar. At root, these stories have the same premise, but the details, characters, settings, conflicts, and plots set them apart. Each writer may start with the exact same idea, but each uses that idea to say something unique, perhaps even wildly different or opposed, based on their worldview. Ideas often overlap, but differences and uniqueness multiply exponentially when ideas are driven on the open road of creativity, which includes sharing ideas, building on connections, and openly relating to common struggles.

Of course, if you're apprehensive about overlap, remember that other writers aren't the *only* ones with story ideas to share. Listen to others, especially people you enjoy having conversations with. I'll bet, as they talk, you'll find sparks that ignite your own creativity. Keep listening, and keep your ears open for ideas you can use and marry with other ideas.

Another reason to seek allies for our writing isn't only to ask them to help brainstorm story ideas. We also need others to weigh in on the story ideas we already have. For instance, say I have what I think is an amazing story idea about a woman who has a passion for helping needy people in Africa. However, my experience with this topic is limited, and in my worldview, I can't imagine anyone who would not love and respect this character. Seeking feedback from friends, though, can broaden what I know and reveal other possibilities. Perhaps one friend has heard bad reports about money being squandered by supposedly helpful mission organizations. Perhaps another reminds me that some countries have shown a poor ability to use relief money to bring positive changes. Maybe another friend feels that foreigners helping in Africa are culturally condescending and full of themselves. All these reactions can spark ideas about how to improve my story and make it more dramatic.

Sympathy and empathy are very individual responses. A particular situation like a wounded dog may tug at your heartstrings, while another person could walk by the same dog and barely notice. It's important to recognize this and search out a variety of responses to your ideas. For example, I have a best friend who is usually one of my early readers for new ideas, but she can't stand reading romance. Even though my novels, more often than not, contain romance, I love the diversity of her point of view. It helps me to see my stories through someone's eyes who does not get swept up in the mushy stuff. I want to know if the rest of my plot holds up enough to engross my friend without relying on the romantic elements.

Taking other people's perspectives into account can help bring a new richness and fullness to your ideas. These new perspectives can identify sources of tension and conflict that you can use in your storytelling. We need allies to improve our ideas.

However, I'd also like to caution you about sharing your

ideas. First, remember that, just because someone has a different perspective, that doesn't mean you have to throw out any ideas, and you aren't required to use the ideas that others offer. In the end, it's always your story.

Plus, ideas can be precious and fragile. Be thoughtful about when, where, and with whom you share your ideas. At times, you will want to brainstorm with a friend or two, but choose these friends carefully, and choose the timing of when you share your ideas wisely. In their early stages of story development, ideas can be tenuous. Sometimes, when we are still exploring, and a particular spark doesn't yet have roots or legs, a simple raised eyebrow from another person, or a negative reaction of any kind, can kill the idea before it has a chance to fully form.

For instance, say you decide to share a brand-new glitzy idea with your mom, since you can always count on her to be excited with you. But your mother didn't sleep well last night, and as you get to the good part, she yawns and nods distractedly. Your excitement shrivels, and even though your mother apologizes for her reaction, you decide to throw out the idea and never actually write it. But what if it truly *was* great?

Protect your ideas initially, even when you're excited, and even when you're convinced they are awe-inspiring. Let ideas grow, so they have a foundation, before sharing. Then, when you do share, start with telling your brainstorming partner that you are excited, and you really don't want that excitement to be dulled. Rather than simply sharing your proposed plot, ask your brainstorming partner what certain elements in your plot make them think of, remember, or feel. If you're writing about a waitress whose daughter has gone missing, ask your allies about any memorable waitresses they've come across. Ask them if they've ever been personally involved with anyone with a missing child, or if they've seen movies with this aspect. Watch their reactions and get their feedback to help you expand on your own ideas. When you do feel ready to share your envisioned plot, remember that you may not know how to fully explain or deliver the idea effectively yet. Take your time to really explain it, build upon the elements your allies already seemed to connect to, and do it justice.

Protecting your ideas while also getting new perspectives and constructive feedback can be tricky. In addition to developing ideas before sharing them, also work hard to find and develop trusted critique allies. As you offer feedback to others on their ideas, model the behavior you'd like to see with your story ideas. Reflect the excitement of others over their ideas while exploring with them new possibilities and expanding on your personal views and experiences with each plot element.

Naturally, choose your idea allies carefully. Consider the personality types of your friends before laying out all of your best story ideas before them. While it may seem natural to approach your most sanguine, extroverted friends if you're looking for an enthusiastic reaction, don't assume such people are always the best audience. Will you get intimidated by a person who takes your idea and runs with it, spouting one great idea after another? In the book *Quiet: The Power of Introverts in a World that Can't Stop Talking*, Susan Cain tells us there is zero connection between extroverts and great ideas, but doesn't it sometimes seem like there is? Extroverts are so loud and excited about any ideas they come up with that they all sound great!

Keep in mind that introverts — which includes many writers — are usually the deep thinkers, the sensitive ones. Everyone has particular strengths, so consider what strengths you need.

Finally, when sharing your ideas, I recommend doing it before your mind is fully made up on how you will implement them. If you're asking people for their contributions, thoughts, and suggestions, which may springboard you in new directions, make sure you're in a flexible place. If you're not in that place, perhaps it's not the right time to share.

People talk about writing being a solo endeavor, but honestly, I don't know that any of my story ideas were mine alone. Certainly, many ideas came from my past, things I overheard, or conversations I had with friends, but every book has also involved brainstorming with others. It's true, too many cooks in the kitchen can spoil the broth, but you are the only real "cook" of your story. It doesn't mean you can't have plenty of tasters. In the end, your story reflects your vision, and you don't have to feel pressured to adopt anyone else's.

My most important advice when it comes to partner or group brainstorming is to always make sharing fun. Have wine. Or cake. Or mochas. Or brainstorm at the beach. What will make the brainstorming session enjoyable for all? What will help you create the fun spirit that keeps ideas flowing?

Put It into Practice

1. One way to develop writing allies is to form lively literary or pop culture discussion groups. Discuss your favorite and least-favorite books and movies, focusing on

what works and what doesn't and what makes everyone passionate. If possible, plan a discussion group for this week, either on Skype or in person.

2. Also, consider the diversity of backgrounds and personalities among your friends and colleagues. Do most people reflect the same age, gender, socioeconomic status, ethnicity, culture, and nationality? Seek allies from different backgrounds, who have different ways of seeing the world, and expand your circle to make it as diverse as possible. This will only expand your understanding of the world and the range of different ideas you'll get. Look for varied feedback to spark new paths of thinking and insight into your ideas. Make a list of people you might share with and the perspectives they might offer.

4. Resonance

*Stories are amazing and powerful because they can resonate
with people depending on their needs and experiences
and speak truths we need to hear in that moment in time.*

— SUE MONK KIDD

Great story ideas fulfill needs in the reader. The right
story can help a child whose parents are divorcing feel like he
is not alone. It can give the man who has worked on the same
garbage truck for forty years a good laugh at the end of the
day, which is what he needs to keep going. A grieving widow
may find in certain characters the friends she needs to help her
during her bereavement. A competitive swimmer may find in
the stories of other athletes the inspiration to give his or her all
to the sport.

Ideas, properly implemented, can deliver understanding
and comfort, solidarity, renewed joy, help processing emotions,
and a host of other benefits. Which brings me back to what I
first said: Ideas are important.

My little S.P.A.R.K. formula goes like this:

Seeking ideas + Passion + help from Allies + Resonance =
Kinetic energy or engagement

There's a reason that resonance does not come at the beginning of the equation. Authentic resonance emerges from the process; it can't be imposed from the outside. If you seek to write stories based only on what's already popular, before checking in with your own idea sparks and passions, you may come up against a couple of problems. First, trends change. What resonates with readers shifts along with the culture. Many a writer learned this lesson in the wake of the Vampire Movement, when hundreds of thousands of writers tried to write "the next *Twilight.*" The problem is, at the onset, no one knew *Twilight* would find such a huge audience, so no one was positioned to catch that same wave. When it comes to publishing, it can take years to bring ideas to the fruition of a finished novel. By the time new vampire stories came out, *Twilight*'s wave of popularity was already cresting, and it crashed down soon after. Riding someone else's wave before it falls is unlikely, if not impossible.

Second, your story idea needs to resonate with yourself before you consider readers. Even if you notice a popular trend early, if the idea isn't something that your creative brain has cooked up on its own in some way, if it doesn't ignite your passion, you likely won't have the steam to take you through all the work that drafting and crafting a published book requires.

Resonance *is* important. Without it, you won't feel compelled to write, and your readers won't feel compelled to read. It is most often discovered, however, once the idea train is in motion. Once you have an arsenal of exciting ideas, it's time to think about what need your story satisfies in readers. Save concerns about which customers you're selling to and how you fit within existing genres until nearer the end. Are there any similarities between your new concept and books that are already out there? Based on what resonates with you, and what you hear resonates with others, what about this new idea might find a strong audience? If you can't think of anything, reconsider your story: Can you build higher stakes or make something big and awful go wrong?

Readers are all individuals and gravitate to different types of stories. One will love a predictable plot, like a category romance, where another wants to be surprised. No story resonates with everyone all the time. Your job is to focus on what resonates with and ignites your passion, which is what will make readers gravitate toward *your* writing. If your strength is telling inspirational athletic stories, then select ideas that play into that strength. If you love spinning complicated plots, do so, and emulate the authors whose plots resonate with you.

And don't stop there! Once you figure out the bigger ideas you're passionate about and how they relate to others, consider all the details of your story. Run character names past friends to see which names make them listen a little closer and which ones make them twist up their faces in distaste. Do your writing allies think the Italian restaurant where most of your scenes are set is too bland? If sharing the details of your Costa Rican setting causes your friend to babble on about how she's always wanted to travel to Costa Rica, then there is your resonance.

Work within your strengths, and figure out how you, specifically, can best connect to the world.

Put It into Practice

1. Get used to using the word *resonance* in your everyday life. Think often about what resonates with you and why. Ask those around you what resonates with them. This week, make it a goal to ask at least five people what kinds of stories resonate most with them.

5. Kinetic Energy

*A lot of my creative energy
is spent coming up with a concept that,
once I get it, I feel like it writes itself.*
— MALLORY ORTBERG

Kinetic energy is energy that a body (in this case, a body of written work) possesses by virtue of being in motion. As you move through the four sections above — seeking ideas, finding your passion, collaborating with allies, and discovering what resonates — your ideas will develop forward motion. As these elements come together, this "kinetic" energy gives your ideas a unique momentum that will carry you through the actual writing of the story and make the process seem almost easy or effortless.

This is also called engagement. Who wants to slog through months or years of forcing yourself to sit down and write a story you've lost interest in? Not me! True, some days will be like that, and there's nothing you can do to prevent your enthusiasm from flagging at times. But wouldn't it be wonderful if on *most* days you could sit down and feel like your book, at least in part, is writing itself?

That's what kinetic energy and engagement are about.

The brain's adaptability makes it possible to find solutions to all questions. All you need is the question, focused energy, and time to let the question percolate. *The Brain That Changes Itself* by Norman Doidge explains the plastic nature of our brains, which are always changing. They are always strengthening in areas we focus on and weakening in areas we neglect.

Once you reach the stage of kinetic energy, no plot problem is a true obstacle to your idea. If the story isn't quite coming together yet, don't worry! Allow yourself time to fill in the blanks. Stay engaged and give yourself the benefit of the doubt. Given time and focused energy, you will come up with the perfect solutions.

Remember, that initial revelatory idea is just the start. The bones of your manuscript and that "wow factor" emerge from the connections between ideas that you make along the way. Maybe the idea of writing about a girl with an eating disorder first made you go aha! But by the end, that girl will be coping with a dying mother who forces her to face the preciousness of life and the palpability of death.

Kinetic energy starts with the first bout of excitement you feel over an idea, and it continues until a reader picks up your book, and even beyond. As we know from ourselves, great stories can affect us for the rest of our lives. Don't you still remember stories you read as a child or teen that have stayed with you? This reaction happens because your brain experienced an emotionally charged moment (or moments) and released plenty of dopamine to increase the memory of those events. When readers are engaged, they mirror or align with the story's kinetic energy. In this way, readers make the story their own, and your story's kinetic energy sustains itself through years and even generations of readers.

The energy that is created when you start brainstorming builds and grows until, with your effort, it amounts to something wonderful. Trust your creativity, and always be working, thinking, brainstorming, and researching. If you rest on one project, start work on another. Keep your creative muscles fired up, and keep the momentum of creativity flowing. Then you never have to force yourself to fight against static inertia.

Ideas build more ideas. Think of ideas like a skyscraper you're building with your mind. Once you have a foundation, it's as if the walls magically build themselves. You blink and they're painted. Suddenly, there's an elevator taking you from the ground-floor ideas to the penthouse view almost instantly, and you can stop at any floor in between and find something interesting and intriguing.

The options are endless! If you put into practice seeking ideas, finding your passion, collaborating with allies, and discovering what resonates, your kinetic energy will grow without any extra work. Trust in the magic of S.P.A.R.K. In part 2, we'll apply these principles to find unlimited sources for ideas and entertaining ways to mine for and implement them.

Part II

Generating Sparks

*Great innovators are a lot like the rest of us.
They procrastinate. They feel doubt and fear.
They have bad ideas.*

— **ADAM GRANT**

Where do you get your story ideas?

Mine come from a variety of places, including movies, dreams, talking to friends and hearing about their lives, social media, waiting in line at the grocery store, and newspaper headlines. All it takes is a spark of an idea, and I'm off and running to see if I can expand it into a novel-length plot.

Plot ideas can come from almost anywhere. Your important task is to learn to keep your eyes and ears open and to figure out where *your* best ideas usually come from.

Brainstorming is a simple but effective skill every writer needs. It's much like a muscle, and the more you build the skill of brainstorming, the easier and more natural it becomes. I recommend brainstorming for five minutes every morning before speaking to another person. It's amazing what our minds can come up with after they've had six or eight hours to percolate in a sleep state, and before we get busy with the rest of our lives. Jot down everything that comes to mind, even in short form, so it doesn't slip away. Here are my five most-important guidelines for brainstorming:

1. There are no bad ideas. Write down every single thing.
2. Your instincts are more important than you usually give them credit for.

3. It is often not a single idea but the connection between two or more ideas that gives us our "aha" moments.
4. Use freewriting or writing prompts when you're stuck.
5. Dream big and wild. Don't limit yourself or feel like you have to be 100 percent "realistic" while brainstorming.

Once you put these guidelines to work in your life, believe me, you will have more than enough ideas! So here's one final piece of advice as you practice building your observational muscles: Keep all of your ideas in one place. Choose a method for corralling the many ideas floating in the atmosphere around you. It could be a notebook you carry with you, your laptop, or a phone app, if you, like me, are tethered to your smartphone 24/7. Just make sure you have some system of logging all of your ideas in one location, so later, when you're ready to use that idea you loved so much, you can easily find it.

Once you have the seed of an exciting idea, spend time thinking about what your story might be at its most basic level. Is it a character against a strong opponent? A character who needs to change and grow? A character waging an internal battle?

Does this story still excite you when you put it into those terms? If so, then keep with it! If your creative juices are telling you that you have something great to work with, get to work on the story itself. For more on developing a story plan, see my book *Fast Fiction* (see endnotes). In the meantime, or when the well runs dry, return to the practices described here.

6. Observational Skills

It is better to ask some of the questions
than to know all the answers.
— JAMES THURBER

I am the perfect person to write about observation
because I was not born with this natural ability. I truly have had
to learn it. You know during political elections when political
parties flood streets and lawns with signs and posters and but-
tons for their candidates? Yes, well, more than once my husband
has asked me who I plan to vote for, and I've replied, "Oh, is
there an election coming up?"

That's how blind I can be to the world around me if I don't
actively practice the skill of observation.

Being a good observer and learning how to catalog the ideas
around you is a little like becoming a collector — but not in
order to fill up your house with useless knickknacks. You become a collector of characters, settings, motives, and obstacles.

To train yourself to be more observant, find something to
open your mind to every day. Foster curiosity. Read something

every day, whether it's a newspaper ad, a poem, a short story, or anything. And actively watch people every day. Write down what you see, what interests you about people or places, and what questions roam in your mind after spending time observing people.

Too much TV is your enemy. It is a constant reminder of what's already been done, and it can end up limiting your mind, even if ideas still have plenty of room for expansion. Watching a TV show, you may suddenly look at your story and think, "My idea is not as good." Or, "I have to do something else because my idea has already been done."

Rather than get caught in comparisons, really practice seeing the world with fresh eyes. My son has a game called Brain-Box. In it, cards show simple pictures, containing several objects, such as a sun, a couple of lawn chairs, and a beach ball. After setting a timer, each player memorizes what's on their card. Then, putting the card aside, upside down, they are asked a question about one of the objects, like, "How many clouds were in the sky?" or "What color were the boy's shorts?"

My son was instantly better at this game than both of his parents. Whether it's his age (twelve) or his natural ability, I don't know, but I do know that you can train yourself to be better at this skill. How do I know? Because over time, I was eventually able to beat my son at this game (at least once or twice!).

To start, resolve to take the time to be open-minded about the world around you. Don't force yourself to always have the answers. Instead, ask questions, notice problems, and be curious. By building up your observational muscles, you'll gain more places and opportunities to find new ideas.

Another suggestion is to set a time limit. No one can observe with intense focus for an extended time, or all the time. The truth is, the shorter your time limit, the more focused you will probably be during that time. Start with five minutes. How many new sights, sounds, touches, and tastes can you notice in five minutes?

Likewise, limit your physical boundaries. Choose one room, one section of a park, or even one person. Don't try to see everything all at once. Focusing on a small area will force you to really concentrate and notice all the small, not-so-obvious details. It can be easy to get distracted or overwhelmed by too many details.

Finally, during your observations, or immediately after, make detailed notes. I encourage you to jot down everything, and circle anything that immediately resonates as something you think you'll one day want to come back to.

When you observe, consider the following questions and ideas:

- Practice really seeing the details around you. Set your watch for a minute or five minutes, look around yourself with purpose, and then when the time is up, close your eyes. How much can you remember?
- Do this with a buddy. One person keeps his or her eyes open and asks the other questions about your surroundings. Practice seeing and noticing all the little details.
- Go somewhere different regularly. Don't just stick to the same routines. Purposefully visit a different coffee shop, restaurant, or gas station. Drive home from work using a different route and sit in a different chair.

Commit yourself to discovering something new in the world every day. To help you, I've provided lists of questions for you to consider when you're out in the world and different prompts about what and how to observe. Don't feel like you have to answer all these questions or do all these things, but consider the ones that raise your interest.

Your Artist's Brain by Carl Purcell tells us to use our visual spatial mind rather than our intellect to view and observe. Try this as you observe people:

- How do objects and people relate to each other in space? Notice the shapes of what is actually before you, not only what you imagine to be there. Don't imagine eyelashes that are actually in shadow. Look for the shapes and details you *can* see. Don't generalize to stereotypes.
- If you had to describe the contour of a person, would it be thick, sharp, and black or soft and gray?
- Squint until that person becomes fuzzy. What stands out now? Don't worry about looking weird. We are writers. We are supposed to be weird.
- Squint to reduce a person to a geometric shape. Are they boxy or very round? Are they triangular?
- Draw the people you find interesting or inspiring. Do this even if you don't consider yourself a talented artist. Notice what you want to draw about them first — their feet? Their head? Their hair? What parts do you draw with confident heavy lines, and in what order do you fill in the details?
- Also draw people from memory. Try closing your eyes

and recalling the important physical details of someone you once knew.

- How much space do the people keep around them? This can reflect a cultural or personal quality. When my husband and I traveled to Romania several years ago, we were sitting on a bench chatting with a local, and another Romanian came along and wiggled his butt right in between us! He filled the gap between us and the local, which seemed completely normal to him. To us North Americans, it didn't feel normal at all.
- Do the people you're observing wear bright colors, or in some other way appear to want to be noticed?
- Do people hide their face behind facial hair, long sweeping bangs, or a hat? Do they carry an object as though it would protect them?
- How do people sit or stand? What's their posture, relaxed or tense?
- Imagine each person in a different setting or emotional state: How might they act in their home, at an office, at a symphony, or attending a baseball game?
- Do certain people have an emotional charge in the air around them?
- Do people exhibit quirks in their body language and facial expressions?
- Age the people you observe. Who will they be and what will they look like in ten years? Thirty?
- Imagine people as children and teenagers.
- Take an imaginary magnifying glass and go closer up. Then closer still. How close can you go?

- Back up like a camera zooming out. Can you imagine someone's family and the rest of his or her world and how they relate to it?

Of course, don't just focus on people. Consider and observe every place you go:

- What will this location be like in fifty years?
- What were the buildings like when they were brand new and first built?
- If you had to pick a center point of this locale, what would it be?
- Pretend you're a photographer, and bring into focus something in the background of this setting. Why did you choose that feature? What is unique or interesting about it?
- In a large location, focus on the smallest details possible. Why is that sock lying in the middle of the street? Where did the smudge on the window come from?
- Look at the scene as if through a small window. Hold up your fingers in an L-frame. What do you notice when you narrow your focus? Can you observe more details?
- Imagine how the setting would look at different times of day, under different lighting. Would it affect the mood? How does that change the way you perceive it?
- What would happen if a natural disaster struck this setting?
- What is the color palette in this setting? What colors stand out? I work regularly on TV and movie sets, and I'm always amazed at how much planning and detail

go into sets to make them look real, and how designers choose color palettes to make the main characters
stand out.

- As with people, draw the setting. Focus first on the
overall silhouette. Take liberties with the lines and make
it as interesting as possible. Could there be a curvy window? A door that seems too small for most people to fit
through?

- Make a drawing in color. What do you most want to
add color to?

- Consider "enhancing" the location in your drawing.
Add nooks, crannies, and hidden "secret" areas. These
add depth, dimension, and interest. Place them anywhere and everywhere. Try to capture the spirit of your
setting, not the exact details.

- As you did with people, draw a setting from memory.
This can be more useful to brainstorming than re-
creating an actual location or even staring at a photo.
Close your eyes and consider what details stick out in
your memory and why.

When you're writing your story, keep all these details in
mind, especially the use of color. Try contrasting character colors with setting colors. What color palette would you assign to
each of your characters? Would this be based on their personality, or on something more external, like their job? As you design
your own setting, keep it visually interesting. Play with color to
distinguish characters and locations. You'll probably find that
red will be remembered, as will gold and silver.

Now, let's focus again on those "main characters."

- Whenever you walk into a coffee shop or grocery store, consider who might be the "main characters" if the scene was a movie in the middle of filming?
- What would only their silhouette tell you about each character?
- How do these characters move? With confidence? Uncertainly? With big or small movements? Don't be afraid to take liberties with these characters and make them larger than life when you make notes about them.
- Who is softer? Who is sharper? See people as an artist would.
- How do people compare in physical size?
- From what you see, what do you imagine would be a person's biggest insecurity? What would be their biggest point of pride?
- What is the energy and mood of each person?
- Compare people to enhance your ideas. Who is smarter? Who is taller? More polished? Better with words?
- Study and observe relationships. How do people interact?
- Based on their appearance and manner, what is each person's biggest conflict? What do they value most?
- Do people have unusual ways of showing friendliness, affection, or annoyance?

Finally, observe with all your senses, not just your eyes.

- What do people sound like? Close your eyes and listen to their voices, of course, but also listen to what sounds their shoes make, the rustle of their clothing, and the sound of their breathing. What do you hear that you don't notice with your eyes open?

- What sounds do you hear in the location? What are the noises that everyone else probably isn't noticing?
- What aromas do you smell around you? Does the location always have the same smell? Is it mild or pungent? Can you separate smells of people, place, and things?
- Close your eyes and feel different items around you. How would you describe them if you couldn't use your eyes? Feel your own skin, your hair, the grass, the weather. Give words to how each item feels.
- Close your eyes and focus on taste. Can you taste a flavor in the air? Really concentrate on each item you eat for lunch one day. Describe the taste and quality of each in a paragraph or even an entire page. Bring the taste to life.

Vincent van Gogh suggested not to paint what you see but what you feel. When you practice observing people and places, notice how you feel. What would you want to make your readers feel about everything you see? Explore the feelings that are present during various events, like parties and funerals. Notice the unusual.

Then use all that you observe as material when you brainstorm your story ideas. Put those observations to work in your writing. As an exercise, choose a physical location to brainstorm, and think of it like your "arena" from *The Hunger Games*. In *The Hunger Games*, the game arenas are specifically designed to create problems and conflict. Now, you are the Game Master. How would you design the "arenas" or settings in your story with the same intent? What would you include that would create conflict and drama?

Use the questions in this chapter as a jumping-off point. Asking questions can have a snowball effect. The question "What if my character got married?" opens up a whole slew of other questions: Where would she marry? Who would she marry? How would their families differ? How would this change her day-to-day life? And so on.

Once you have garnered a few ideas you like, don't stop there. Coming up with a new idea can be a little like buying a car. When I had a red Toyota RAV4, suddenly I saw red Toyota RAV4s *everywhere*. Some had spoilers, and some had different-colored door handles. Some of them had a redundant spare tire on the back, while others must have had spare tires inside the car. Plus, each RAV4 had a different driver and was on a trek to somewhere different than I was.

Once you have an idea, use your newly pumped-up observation muscles to notice where else this idea appears in the world. What's different and the same about it in these other situations? Keep brainstorming as many ideas as possible. Asking your mind for more ideas often makes the process easier, not harder, because as your mind comes up with multiple ideas, there's a lot less pressure on each individual idea to perform. Instead of asking yourself for one great idea when you visit a coffee shop or grocery store, ask yourself for twenty-five ideas of all kinds. Don't allow yourself to be satisfied with the first idea that comes to mind.

Exercise your observational muscles regularly to make them stronger and to make the process of mining ideas effortless. If you work at this once per year, it won't come easily. But work at it every day, and you will get stronger quickly.

My final piece of advice is to regard each observation you make as valuable. Suspend your disbelief. Perhaps this person in front of you, this location you're standing in, could inspire the perfect character or setting for a breakout new novel. Give each idea a fighting chance to find its way into one of your stories.

7. Fun and Games

*Creative ideas flourish best in a shop which preserves
some spirit of fun. Nobody is in business for fun,
but that does not mean there cannot be fun in business.*

— LEO BURNETT

Is it your understanding that kids play and adults work? Is that your paradigm? If so, it's time to change it! Carving out time simply to brainstorm ideas in a world that esteems multitasking and busyness can be a hard mental jump to make, so I've made each game quick and easy to do. I titled this chapter "Fun and Games" because I believe that's the spirit to adopt when looking for story ideas. How would it have felt if I'd called these "exercises"? Like work, right? But who needs more *work* in their life? Approaching idea creation like work puts you in the wrong frame of mind.

Writing stories is a messy craft, using dirt and mud and clay, rather than a too-neat process. Many writers get intimidated or overwhelmed by the prim blank page. Being perfectionists, they don't want to mess it up, which puts too much pressure on the poor struggling-to-be-creative writer. Instead, treat a blank page like a sandbox or a mud puddle. I encourage you to be a kid for a while and play. You can come inside and clean up later.

Remember those carnival fun house mazes you navigated through as a kid? You thought it would be easy, but suddenly you were in the middle of a box of mirrored walls with seemingly no exit. Writing stories can be like that sometimes, and generating new ideas is your way of getting out of the maze. Oh, where there had been a mirror, suddenly there's an exit! And wait, now there are two, then three more. Which one will you choose?

The fun of storytelling is that you can choose *all* the exits. Choose them all and see where each goes, and only then decide which route is the best one to get you out. Maybe it won't be the fastest or the easiest route (it probably shouldn't be), but it will certainly be the most entertaining route. It'll be the one that's made you think in new ways and surprises the reader.

In the end, each idea or exit in your story should feel like the perfect solution. But sometimes you can't know which is the perfect solution until you try all of them. This section provides the tools for coming up with new ideas and endless routes to choose from. Read on.

The Fast Five

To begin searching for story ideas, here are five fun and fast ways to get your brainstorming muscles pumping:

1. Skim your local newspaper headlines. You don't have to read the articles. Just see if any headlines capture your attention.

2. Chat with friends. Ask them what interesting things have happened lately or what is the *most* interesting thing that's ever happened to them.

3. Skim your Twitter or Facebook feeds. Could any posts make for interesting character traits, motivations, or plot obstacles?

4. Ask a friend to provide you with a character prompt, such as a name or a heroic quality. Write this seed in the middle of a blank page, and then add everything that comes to mind around it (see "Idea Map" next).

5. At a store or restaurant, observe a server or clerk, note their name on their name tag, and then go home and write an imagined life for that person.

Idea Map

A blank page inhibits ideas, but all it takes is one word to change a blank page from inhibiting to inspiring! Write one word, any word, in the middle of a blank page, and then write around that word absolutely everything that comes to mind when you think of it. How many ideas does the word *trophy* spark for you? Write it all down, and you no longer have a blank page. Rather, you have an idea map, or a thought cloud, where you can search for ideas that will feed your stories. This is a great way to spark connections between two or more unrelated ideas that, together, become something fresh and interesting. From there, ideas and plots can snowball.

For example, in the middle of a page, write the word *jar* (or pick any common household object), and come up with as many uses for that object as possible. What could a jar hold besides jam? At first you may find it difficult to brainstorm, but as you come up with your first idea, and then your second, you'll notice it gets easier and easier. Eventually you'll move from the obvious to the obscure. Your jar might be used for a twine dispenser or a plant holder or a chandelier. The more ideas you get, the more you'll get after that.

Now take the glass you are drinking out of, or the pen you are holding, or a stool or a book. What else could these things be used for? Shoot for at least a hundred other uses for each object.

Now consider everything you've written, and choose just one use for that common object that looks interesting. Write this main idea in the middle of another large blank page, and create an idea map for this interesting usage. As ideas collect around the page, sprout off lines to connect ideas that lead to or relate to other ideas. What plot and character ideas come to mind? Who would use this item in the way you are suggesting, and why? Are you discovering new characters that could be useful in a story? Write down everything you are imagining about them.

Name Storm

What is in a name? A lot, actually. Recently, I was reflecting on what is involved in creating memorable characters, and I thought about the fictional characters who remain the most memorable to me. On thinking about why these characters are memorable, I noticed one interesting component: Characters whose names I could easily remember automatically felt closer to my heart than characters I remembered loving but whose names I struggled to recall.

Why does remembering a character's name make them automatically more memorable in every way? I decided it's because they become more personal, and they often feel almost like friends — as though I had been on their journey with them. I read about a hundred books a year, and most of them I couldn't tell you the first name of the main character after about a week. I've never considered this a problem, but I think it might be. Even though I enjoyed many of those books while reading them, today I can't tell you much about the characters or the plot.

So how do you come up with memorable names? One of my favorite characters is Anna in Stephanie Perkins's novel *Anna and the French Kiss*. As if having Anna's name in the title wasn't enough to make it memorable, Anna's best friend is constantly sending her bananas (while Anna sends her friend Bridget bridges), and if *that* wasn't enough, her name was secured, at least for me, when the hot British boy with fantastic hair pronounced her name in a very special way.

But is a memorable name enough to make a character memorable? Probably not. Anna also has a witty and fantastic voice. Both are probably essential. I honestly don't know if Anna's voice would be enough to bring her, specifically, to mind, if I didn't also easily recall her name and feel like I've been on her journey alongside her.

In part, character names become memorable when they are significant to the characters themselves, and I've always unthinkingly employed at least one small device to help readers remember each of my main character's first names. With Brie in *Losing Faith*, she talks about how her parents named her after a cheese because she's the cheesy daughter. Loann in *Never Enough* breaks her name down into two parts: Lo and Ann. Lo for the low man on the totem pole, and Ann as the plain-Jane name that she thinks suits her perfectly. In *Foreign Exchange*, the hot neighbor boy calls Jamie "James," which makes her think she'll always be like a brother to him. And in *A Christmas Kerril*, Kerril is the title character, who feels like she gets ridiculed for her name around Christmastime.

I considered why Katniss Everdeen is so memorable. First, in a world where everyone is looking out for themselves, it's automatically noteworthy for a character to act and think so selflessly. As for her name, I think the cute "Catnip" nickname definitely helped.

In this day and age, many names have become gender neutral. Many names that were common twenty years ago now seem either old-fashioned or in vogue again. I encourage you, as you come across different character names that interest you, to consider what makes the name appealing for you and what will make it memorable for your readers.

To play around with name brainstorming, list five names that interest you. Vary the length and the first letter or first sound of each name to make a well-rounded cast that won't get confused. Then go through each name individually and come up with a nickname, mispronunciation, character quality, or story behind the name that could make this name memorable for your readers.

When you're done with your five names, keep an ongoing list of names you find interesting or appealing and discover ways to make them memorable in your spare time.

Fill-in-the-Blank Logline

You may have heard of the term *elevator pitch*, which is basically a one-to-two-sentence description of your novel. This is meant to be a synopsis so snappy you can pitch it to an editor or agent in an elevator ride. A *logline* is the term screenwriters use for the same thing.

In this game, you use a fill-in-the-blank logline to create a similar pithy story idea.

"But wait!" I can hear some of you say. "I can't write a logline yet! I don't know what my story is about! That's why I'm reading this book!"

Fair enough. And you will use the bones of an empty logline to discover that story.

I was fortunate enough to take a workshop on loglines and story pitches with veteran Hollywood producer and screenwriter Luke Ryan, and he shared the empty frame he uses to create loglines for his movies.

Take a moment to look over the frame. Use a notebook to jot down the frame, leaving empty spaces, or print a copy from my website at http://www.denisejaden.com/loglineframe.

_____

(Write your character's name)

Sets out to _____
(Write your character's goal)

But runs into _____
(Write a physically and/or psychologically devastating obstacle)

And must _____
(Write how your character will overcome this or be changed)

Let's break it down line by line, and write on your blank logline frames as you go.

Start with your main character's name.

Spend a few minutes brainstorming interesting names, as in the previous exercise. If you wish, flip to the appendix for further inspiration. Don't worry about carefully choosing the perfect name. Just go with whatever name grabs you or appeals to you.

For this example, I'll use the name Henry. I could stop with just a first name, but I'll choose a surname as well, which helps flesh out this character. I'll give Henry the surname Hernandez, and I'll also give him a couple of descriptive qualities — one physical characteristic and one emotional/personality characteristic.

In the logline's first blank, I write: "Shy and lanky Henry Hernandez."

Consider the next two logline blanks together. Consider your character's main motivation at the same time that you come up with your character's main obstacle. It's fun to brainstorm these together because that way you can choose an ironic obstacle that really stokes your creative fire.

For example, I imagine that Henry Hernandez would have

an extreme fear of heights, so some interesting goals might be saving a princess from a tall tower, having to fly a small airplane over open waters to save the world, or bungee jumping with his boss in order to earn a much-desired promotion. The obstacle does not have to be ironic, but irony may lend some immediate ideas, and it will pack a punch if a character's goal connects to something powerful in terms of the character's limitations. Make this obstacle as devastating both physically and psychologically as possible for your character. If you get stuck, peruse the appendixes for help, and remember that you can build and refine the stakes and goals later if you choose to develop this story.

Finally, consider the fourth blank line: What would be the most satisfying resolution? Do I imagine that Henry Hernandez will attain his goal, or will he realize through his tenacity that a different goal would be more suited to him and his life? In other books and movies, what endings have really resonated with you? Did you like happy, feel-good resolutions or ones that provide a jolt of surprise? Did you prefer seeing characters find the inner strength to overcome their obstacles? Choose the type of ending that motivates and energizes you, and write it in for the character you've imagined.

Now, consider the logline you just created. Does it resonate with you? Do you have a favorite part? Do you feel particularly connected to this character? Do you feel urged on by his or her goal, or do your palms sweat at the thought of the obstacle? Does the ending send chills or shivers or butterflies through your system?

Maybe not, and if not, that's okay. Remember, this is just playing around. It's nothing serious. It's simply one way to jump-start your creativity when you're blocked for ideas. Perhaps only one part of your logline resonates with you, and if so, keep that and change the rest. Or expand on the logline further and see if by adding additional details you start to feel more connected to the story. Consider adding a location or setting that makes the dilemma more interesting. Nothing is set in stone. Enjoy the creative process and see where it leads. Keep what works for you, and save the rest in a "Not for Now" folder.

Of course, this is also an excellent activity if you've already got a story in mind. My critique partner, Rachel Shane, even takes this one step further and writes query letter–like blurbs once her story components start to come together. She finds that the act of trying to get the main plot arc into a one-paragraph "pitch" helps her see the strength of her ideas or nail down lacking elements. She also finds that once she is in the zone for writing these blurbs, she can write several at once. After writing the first one, the following blurbs come easier and easier.

Remember, when you're stuck for ideas for the fill-in-the-blank logline frame, peruse the appendixes for missing story elements, or start dividing your own brainstormed ideas into categories that will correspond to the logline frame — characters, motives, and obstacles — and you'll never be stuck without the essential elements for a new story.

Thematic Inspiration

What kinds of story themes excite you? That's a very big question in a small number of words, isn't it? Maybe even contemplating story themes brings back horrific flashbacks from high school

English. For me, themes were elusive and vague, and meanings seemed to change endlessly depending on whom I spoke with. Still, I've changed, and now I like to play games with themes to help brainstorm new stories. I promise this won't be scary. This is in the "Fun and Games" chapter, after all!

To me, at its most basic, a theme is the word or group of words that resonates with you after a story is finished. It names what the story is about. It could be the life lesson learned by the main character. This does not have to be a moral lesson, but it might embody a truism, like "blood is thicker than water."

"But wait," I hear you saying. "I don't have a story, so how can I have a theme, and what if I don't know how to identify themes, anyway?"

Again, fair enough. This game not only helps you brainstorm stories, but it helps you learn how to identify themes.

Review the list of seven one-word themes below. As you do, think of a favorite book or movie and identify which theme matches your book or movie the best.

Seven Simple Themes

1. Love
2. Faith
3. Forgiveness
4. Trust
5. Survival
6. Honor
7. Acceptance

Did one of these fit your favorite story? If so, great! Now pick another favorite book or movie, and repeat the process. Do this at least five times, and see if one theme word seems to come up more often than others. If so, use that theme to brainstorm a new story, or choose one of the themes that illuminates for you. I discuss this in more detail next.

If you didn't find a theme in this list that matched your favorite book or movie, that's fine, too. Simply think of other books and movies and try to find matches. This list isn't meant to be comprehensive. Depending on whom you talk to, all stories basically boil down to ten or twenty themes, while some say there are in fact hundreds of different story themes. In the appendix, I've provided a much longer list of themes to help with brainstorming, and you can use that list for this game as well.

If you use the theme list in the appendix, here's another strategy: Read through the list and circle the themes that resonate with you or make you pause and think, "I'd like to read a story about that!" Circle as many as you like, and then spend a few minutes considering each one and simply visualizing a possible story where that theme could come into play.

Once you've identified a theme you like, envision what kinds of characters would occupy that story. Hint: It's great to use some irony when brainstorming characters from a theme. For example, if the theme "acceptance" illuminates for you, think of a type of character who may be refusing to accept something about him- or herself, something that is in complete opposition to his or her sense of self. For instance, perhaps a drill sergeant has worked his way up in the ranks of the army, but he has always felt an inner pull toward working with kids.

Try this game right now. Consider the themes that your favorite books or movies embody, and then brainstorm your own plots and characters.

Brainstorm like a Child

I live in British Columbia and homeschool my son. Recently, our province's educational system made a fairly drastic change away from test-based grading. They want teachers to focus more on project-based learning and allowing students to ask, and answer, many of their own questions.

This highlighted for me how much we have strayed from respecting the perspective and questions of children. Children question everything, and their minds are flexible; they see all sorts of solutions and answers. They ask "what if?"

But in our society, adults like things the way they are. They learn clear, correct answers, and if they don't know something, Google has the answer at their fingertips. As children grow, they are taught to memorize correct answers, and only correct answers are rewarded. There is no space on the test for other responses and good questions.

The truth is, problems, or things that we *don't* know, can spark great ideas. So I encourage you to dig deeper than the obvious, memorized, Googled answers. Search out other possibilities. In other words, practice brainstorming like a child.

This is more difficult than it sounds. It means observing the world as if everything is new, unlearned, unmemorized. It means living with a sense of wonder, rather than clinging to our learned understandings and correct knowledge. For instance, in *Wild Ideas — Let Nature Inspire Your Thinking*, Elin Kelsey tells a story of squirrels who learn how to cross the street in busy traffic by watching people, not by being told what to do. Kelsey encourages children to "squirrel it out" when solving problems. You can do the same: Don't assume you know, but learn by observing what others do. Learn by asking, "What's new and exciting in the world today?" Let your mind see your surroundings as filled with possibility.

Here are some fun suggestions to get you started in retraining your mind to brainstorm like a child:

- When my best friend's son started speaking, two of his first words were "What's that?" He said them so often, pointing at everything, that they ran together into one word: *Whatsat? Whatsat? Whatsat?* My friend patiently answered every single time. She loved his curiosity about the world. I did, too. When he grew to speaking full sentences, he would ask if the wrapped hay bales on roadside farms were giant marshmallows, and it reminded us of how to see through wondrous young eyes. Practice seeing the world around you with a sense of wonder and not knowing. Point to everything and ask, "Whatsat?"

- Spend some time brainstorming outside in nature. Take notice of all five of your senses. Close your eyes. What can you hear? How many objects might make those sounds? Imagine you're not actually where you are, but someplace else. Where could you be? Open your eyes and pretend you have a magic paintbrush and can change anything in new and crazy ways. What would you change?

- Walk through your house like a stranger, or better yet, crawl. Notice the smallest details, like markings on the floor, and imagine where they originated from. Write down all of the details you can find that you've never actively noticed before.

- Children have a knack for answering a question with a question, and a local improvisation troupe has turned this into an improv game, which is always fun. Play the game of questions with a friend, in which you both can *only* converse in questions. Buzz each other if you mess up, and see where it leads you. Practice asking questions rather than dwelling in the state we're used to — shutting up unless we have the answers.

Learn to ask questions constantly, and the answers may give you many new out-of-the-box ideas.

Brainstorm like a Teenager

When I suggest brainstorming like a teen, I'll bet your first thought is: Wouldn't a teen just look up all the answers on Google?

This might be true, but problem solving isn't why I suggest emulating teens. Rather, what defines the teenage years more than any other age?

Teenagers are passionate, and they are often willing to go against the grain.

These are fantastic traits to have as a brainstormer looking for story ideas. As adults, we tend to be realistic and reasonable, and we come up with reasonable ideas and characters. We limit our imaginations and err on the side of dulling our ideas down and lose their larger-than-life qualities.

So, regain the passion and rebelliousness of a teenager when it comes to your brainstorming. Here are a few places to start:

- Watch a movie featuring teen characters this week. Spend some time comparing and contrasting how the teen characters might act or think differently if they were adults. Then, spend a day trying to do the opposite: Think of how you might act or think differently if you were a teen.

- Choose a character you have already brainstormed. Imagine the most unexpected thing that character could do. What would they be willing to go to jail for? What, or who, might they be willing to die for?

- Practice breaking some rules in your stories. In everyday life, we feel obligated not to park where the sign says NO PARKING. We try to be on time for work and to pay for our groceries. But what if you didn't do any of these things? Or, rather, what if *your characters* didn't? Watching characters break rules is part of the excitement of reading fiction, and teenagers can be especially good at this. Take some time to explore the possibilities of breaking real-world rules and imagining the consequences. This is another great way to find added conflict for your stories.

Brainstorm like a Senior Citizen

Now it's time to brainstorm like a senior citizen! First, ask yourself, what do you see as the strengths of the older generation?

To me, the older generation is defined by their understanding of the world, their experience, and their sense of nostalgia. Their many years of being alive have given them many ways to compare and contrast everything they encounter. They have the widest perspective.

Here are two ways to brainstorm like a senior citizen:

- Consider a simple character motivation, like materialism (see Appendix C for more). Now, pretend you are a senior citizen who has seen plenty of materialism in his or her long life. Let this inner senior citizen tell stories about materialism that display a depth of understanding. Perhaps they will tell a childhood story of stealing a toy car from the corner store, and then how they worked to provide all the luxuries for their own children. What insight does your senior citizen share?

- Think of something that you're nostalgic for. Write a paragraph or two about your fond memories. When you're finished, take note of any difference in your feelings or outlook. Would you write differently now, in this state, than you would have before delving into your nostalgia?

When you're done brainstorming like a senior citizen, try imagining some of your favorite characters from books or movies as different ages. For example, try envisioning Batman as a senior citizen, or Scarlett O'Hara as a small child. Try this with some of your own characters, too. Does imagining characters as different ages add variety in your brainstorming?

Movie Inspiration

My husband is a real movie buff, and he is forever encouraging me to watch movies with him. While I enjoy a good movie once in a while, I'm too goal-driven to spend the kind of time he would like me to zoning out in front of the TV.

As a compromise, I came up with a game, of sorts, for myself, so I can keep him company while feeling like the time spent is worthwhile for my creative side. Here's how it works:

When you watch a movie and find yourself enjoying a certain character, make a note of some adjectives that describe what, specifically, you enjoy about this character. Keep an ongoing "Character Adjective List," in your notebook or on an app, and add to the list every time you come across a character you really like.

Over time, see if there are words like *resourceful, witty,* or *selfless* that come up again and again. This will be a good list to draw from when it comes time to create and develop your own characters.

Conversely, when coming across characters that rub you the wrong way, make note of the adjectives that describe the qualities you dislike, and keep these in mind as the types of characters you may want to avoid in your own stories.

Do you find the setting of a certain movie transporting or captivating? Put into a few words why you are taken with it, so it can inspire settings in your own work.

Movie plot points can also make for great inspiration. When you find yourself on the edge of your seat, or highly interested in what will happen next in a movie, jot down the character motives and obstacles that keep you interested.

Take notice of what, specifically, you enjoy in other people's creative work as a way to inspire your own work.

What If...

To generate new ideas for stories and characters, ask "what if" about everything. Always reach further, increasing the radius of your ideas. How big can an idea get? How extreme can you make it without breaking the suspension of disbelief? What if an everyday situation were slightly changed? What adds conflict? What adds excitement? What increases the stakes? What would make a character's life harder?

Once I have a story idea that's coming together, I like to ask these "what if" questions: *What if* things got worse? And worse yet? Then how could they become worse still?

To get ideas flowing, try these "what if" scenarios:

- *What if* a character was seven feet tall? How would that affect his or her life, for better and worse? What conflicts, unease, and benefits might a character experience? Conversely, what if an adult character was under four feet tall?
- *What if* a character was deathly allergic to dust or plants or flowers or cigarette smoke? What conflicts and stories might result?
- *What if* it didn't stop raining for over a year? How would that affect the terrain, people's attitudes, and how they lived their lives?
- *What if* a person transformed into an animal? How would being an animal change the person, and how would the person change the animal? What would result from this mix of traits and selves?
- *What if* a snowstorm drove a random collection of characters to seek shelter together — say, a musician, a plumber, and a seeing-eye dog?
- *What if* a million dollars was dumped into a character's lap? How would things change immediately? How would his or her life look ten years later?
- *What if* a boss had to hire a new assistant? How many types of personality clashes can you think of? How many ways could this relationship change both lives?

Cut, Chop, and Combine

If you've ever seen the cooking show *Chopped*, you can probably guess why the show is so popular. Contestants are forced to take four odd, mismatched ingredients and *make* them work together in a delicious dish. Why not try this with your writing? The process of forcing ideas to work together automatically bolsters creativity.

Once you have a nice collection of ideas using some of the other games, pick two at random and write a story premise that includes both. Try it several times, and try combining three, four, or even five ideas at random. Force yourself to do it, even if what you come up with is ridiculous. If you find this difficult, imagine that the consequences are high. Imagine that you'd win a million dollars if you created the best story out of an odd, mismatched combination of ideas. Or, imagine you would lose your car or your house if you didn't combine the ideas. I'll bet you could do it, and I'll bet you'll find more creativity buried within you than you ever imagined.

Once you have several combined ideas, take the best one and expand on it. Add more details, and flesh out the characters and plot in a way that might really work. How would you organize the story?

This is a game you can play anytime. Whenever you have five spare minutes, flip through your pages of ideas, pick several at random, and see what connections arise between them. Often our aha moments arise not from getting one Great New Idea, but rather when we combine common ideas in new ways that work seamlessly together and provide a fresher take on the original. In our lives today, working long hours and living by our to-do lists, we often think very linearly and with a single-minded focus. This game breaks us free of our ruts.

Another way to create new ideas is to combine two or more

existing stories, whether from books or movies. In her online course on coming up with high-concept story ideas, author Jessica Brody cites that Hollywood and the publishing industry love the idea of mishmashing two existing works, such as two current blockbuster movies, because they are instantly familiar. These professionals can easily envision how to pitch and sell the new story to the public.

Take two ideas and change the details as much as you like, or take one idea and twist it so it becomes fresh and new. Don't plagiarize, of course, but use an already great idea for inspiration. Ask a lot of "what if" questions. What if the main character in *Harry Potter* was a girl? What if you mashed up *Tombstone* with *Rambo*? Or *The Fast and the Furious* with *Grumpy Old Men*? What if you reset *When Harry Met Sally* a hundred years in the past, when the theme of "Men and women can never be friends" would create a whole new set of obstacles? What if the lead character in *Dirty Harry* was a teenage girl? Bam! You have a fresh story that I promise will be nothing like the original.

Brainstorm mashups of your own favorite books and movies. Or try changing the genre of a story. What if your favorite comedy was a horror movie, and vice versa? You can also try the technique my critique partner Rachel Shane uses: Write movie names on slips of paper, along with a list of genres, and throw them into a hat. No matter which two you pick at random, find a way to make them work together.

Part III

Developing the Flame

I find getting the first draft down to be the biggest challenge. Every word, every punctuation mark, every plot point is a decision. It's much more fun to play with something that already exists.

— CYNTHIA LEITICH SMITH

After playing all the fun games in the previous chapter, you will have generated lots of new character and story ideas. You may not feel confident that any of them describe the next story you must write, and that's okay.

In this part, we're going to work on developing the flame, or finessing those ideas into a cohesive and compelling story. We'll talk about choosing and assessing your ideas to figure out how to develop a story you want to write. We'll also talk about following through and how the best story ideas in the world are worthless unless someone fleshes them out into a complete story. I'll offer specific tactics to ensure that once you have a story to write, a story that interests you, you'll stay motivated to do the work and finish it. And, finally, I'll offer some trouble-shooting tips to help you along if you're facing specific problems with your story development.

8. Choosing an Idea

Creativity is allowing yourself to make mistakes.
Art is knowing which ones to keep.

— SCOTT ADAMS

Brainstorming lists of new and exciting ideas is a lot of fun, but now that you have pages and files full of them, you have a new problem. How on earth will you choose between them?

There are several ways to solve this problem. First, always go with your gut. Trust the tiny (or loud) voice inside telling you which idea is the most interesting or compelling to you right now. Follow that voice until it tells you something different.

If your gut really isn't telling you anything, you can also try the Russian roulette method. Cut up a bunch of possible ideas on tiny slips of paper, turn them facedown, mix them up, and then pick one. There you go. Give that one a try!

Don't believe in serendipity quite that much? Yeah, me neither. Here's another option: Take those slips of paper and pick them up two at a time. Compare only those two, and ask yourself, if you had to pick the idea you preferred — if your life or your child's life depended on it — which would you choose? If you still have trouble deciding, ask yourself which would be the easiest or the most fun to implement. You might also ask which idea fits the current marketing trends and pick the opposite one. As I've said, never chase a trend.

Once you've chosen between the first two ideas, discard the rejected slip, and move on to another pair. Keep choosing between pairs of ideas, round-robin style, until you have only one idea left in your hand. Give that one a try. What's the worst that can happen? To foster some creative energy, use the idea to make an "idea map" (see page 53).

Sometimes having too many brilliant ideas can overwhelm us, and we need to simplify our choices. If, now that your ideas are spread out before you, they all seem mediocre, then return to the idea-generating activities in part 2. Keep seeing in new ways till something exciting strikes. Also, as I say, combining ideas often leads to exciting discoveries. Keep combining your favorite ideas until you have a story!

This is why I suggest that quantity is more important than quality when it comes to brainstorming. You want lots of ideas to select from and compare. Don't jump in with both feet the second you have one workable idea. Grab more ideas, and more after that. Harness them. Group them. Compare them. The first idea may not be the best. It may not go as far as you need it to, but it may be the start of something great once other ideas come into play.

You might also compare one of your ideas to something similar that's already been done. How is your idea the same?

How is it different? How is it better? How is the conflict stronger? Can it be made even stronger than that?

Does your idea have an analogy in the real world? Does the struggle in your story mimic a wrestling match? Does the conflict mirror the tension when a person is trying to work up the courage to jump out of an airplane? What, in real life, reminds you of the *feeling* of your story idea?

This same process applies to both plot and character ideas. These go hand in hand, of course. What kind of character excites you? Scan over your list of character names or descriptions: Which ones draw your eye? Combine and shuffle your favorite character ideas with your favorite plot ideas: Which make the most interesting fit?

Ultimately, the right main character is the one who fits the focus of your story. I love the choice of the main character in the movie *Tomorrowland*, which is about how pessimism is literally causing the end of the world. The character is the correct choice because she's both a science geek and an optimist, and both are required to break through and resolve the plot's main conflict. Why is the character you've chosen the right one? Put this into words, and use this for inspiration to counter any self-doubt as you start writing your story.

9. Following Through

*The only way to know that you've gone far enough
is to go too far.*

— JACK FOSTER

Once you have put the work into brainstorming a million ideas, once you have gone through and carefully selected one or ten or a hundred of your ideas that work well together, the hard part is done. You have a story. Following through is simply this: making a deal with yourself that you will do the work, day after day, until the story is completed, even when you don't feel like it, or even when your ideas no longer look as shiny as they once did.

This brings us back to our original motivation for writing. What is the spark that inspires us? Let's take stock of why we write to begin with. After all, why else brainstorm story ideas and try to write a new story that's never been written before?

Here are some of my reasons:

- To taste the thrill of accomplishment
- To connect with people

- To help people
- To entertain people
- To make people laugh
- To enlighten readers
- To reveal myself
- To enjoy bragging rights
- To finish this life well, having been known and exposed and enjoyed

What are some of your reasons for wanting to write a story? Are any of your reasons the same as mine? Make your own list and write it down now.

Rewards and Consequences

We've talked a little about rewards and consequences. Now it's time to decide: When it comes to following through, what is going to motivate you best, an awful consequence or a tempting reward?

One year when I was getting ready to perform on a cruise ship with my Polynesian dance troupe, my husband watched my plans to lose a little weight stagnate, and he made a deal with me. He snapped a few pictures of the flab I was not happy with poking out from around my bikini, and he told me if I didn't reach my goal weight before leaving for the cruise ship, he would post these unflattering pictures on Facebook. Now this is extreme, and my husband is a personal trainer, so he has plenty of experience with putting fires under people's butts in order to make physical changes, but I ask you... would this have worked for you?

And if not, what would?

If you knew the minute you typed "The End" on your story that you could go out and drop three hundred dollars on a new pair of Fluevog shoes, would that motivate you to push through? What if the consequence for not completing your novel was giving up chocolate for six months? The truth is, there has to be *something* that gives you a little extra push, since there will be times that it doesn't feel worth it. There will definitely be days that you don't feel like writing, and you don't know if your story is worthwhile.

Do you work better with rewards for good behavior or consequences for bad? For me, the reward has to be pretty awesome, like a trip to Tahiti, to motivate me. Consequences only have to be minor, like not letting myself eat anything until I've come up with ten new story ideas. (I *can't* go without eating, so this one really works well for me. There has not been a time that I haven't come up with ten ideas, quite quickly, actually!)

The thing with rewards and consequences is that you have to stick to them. If you promise yourself those new shoes, you *must* buy those new shoes as soon as you meet your goal. Make yourself accountable to someone close, and be sure to share both your goal completion date and your planned rewards or consequences.

Maintain Perspective

Pulling your ideas together into a finished story does not mean they're going to be perfect. But would you rather regret writing a book that isn't perfect, or regret never having written a book at all?

When you question your story ideas or your ability as a writer, let those questions fuel the positivity of your characters. Show your characters facing fears or standing up for something they believe in, and soon you'll find those same qualities in yourself again.

Don't be afraid of questions (or leaving blank spaces that you don't know quite how to fill in yet). We have never been in a better position, technologically, to be able to find answers, so have faith that you will come up with all the answers you need — on the second draft. During the first draft, push through and finish.

A trick my first editor at Simon & Schuster, Anica Rissi, taught me for following through was to stop while the going is good. Instead of trying to push through and finish a chapter or flesh out an idea fully, make note of what comes easily, and then put the story completely aside while you're in the middle of a section of writing you're excited about. It's in our nature to want to finish sections and keep pushing through until we're all out of steam, or until we're out of ideas about what to do next. But sometimes it's better to stop writing sooner than that. Don't think about your story or seek solutions constantly, but instead let ideas and solutions simmer in the back of your mind. If you spend time stressing or worrying about your ideas, they will likely be halted in their tracks.

Remember, stories are important. Your ideas are important.

When we think of "inventions," we think of Thomas Edison and Alexander Graham Bell, but what about the Austrian monks who came up with the idea of restaurants? What if Malatesta Novello had never come up with the idea of a public library?

Or maybe more importantly, what if Ignaz Semmelweis hadn't thought of the concept of hand-washing in hospitals?

Who is to say that all this brainstorming won't lead to some brand-new concept that could change the world? Maybe your stories won't invent the lightbulb, but they are capable of sparking ideas in others that could lead to so-far-unthought-of ideas. Did you know the concept of alien abduction hadn't been publicly considered until an influx of science fiction in the 1950s started people thinking about worlds beyond our own?

In some way, we are always changing the world when we write, publish, and participate in culture. Even a meme on Facebook, according to Robert Arp in *1001 Ideas That Changed the Way We Think*, is "an element that guides cultural evolution."

Perhaps you're already guiding our culture without even knowing it.

Find Accountability

NaNoWriMo — National Novel Writing Month — is the great brainchild of author Chris Baty. It's an annual challenge to write a fifty-thousand-word novel during the month of November. Baty's hypothesis is that writers need ambitious goals — so ambitious that they don't have time to take breaks, hesitate, or overthink their work.

Hundreds of thousands of people love to take part in NaNoWriMo year after year, and I've written almost a dozen novels through this yearly challenge, but the NaNoWriMo challenge may not be right for every writer. Why does it work for me and other people? Here are some of the positive aspects writers should consider, whether they jump into the challenge headfirst or not:

1. A short deadline works to spur on many writers. How many people have you met that started a novel ten years ago, but never finished it? There's nothing worse than that sense of unfinished business, and even failure, hanging over a writer to stall him in his path. Setting a short deadline will almost certainly help you get much closer to completion, if not all the way there.

2. Many writers procrastinate because their goals lack ambition. Planning to write one chapter this month may produce small results, but it also may make you a little crazy as you overanalyze every word and as self-doubt sets in on every sentence.

3. Yes, writing is a solo sport, but I don't know a single writer who would say they can complete publishable works all on their own. The nice thing about the NaNoWriMo challenge is that it has a built-in system of camaraderie — a buddy system. But, truly, you don't need NaNoWriMo for their buddy system; just make sure to build your own. My biggest community of writers spur each other on with Facebook. Find something that works for you and stay regular with it.

4. A combination of the short deadline and the ambitious goal works well to create forward momentum with your writing. Do you struggle to find time and mental focus to sit down every day and write? Finding a regular time I can pencil into my schedule for the next year would definitely be a struggle, but deciding that next month

I'll take thirty days to make some leaps and bounds in my writing is much more doable, and I even find people in my life willing to help me make the time. Perhaps you should try giving yourself a short deadline or an ambitious goal, or both, to help spur you on.

5. The thing I love the most about NaNoWriMo is how I sail through the month without spending any time judging my ideas or wallowing in self-doubt. The process of NaNoWriMo kicks my perfectionist nature to the curb. While I would have absolutely nothing publishable to show the world if I lived only in that free-wheeling, momentum-building space, and I didn't take time to later polish my work, it is a great help in the early stages of writing to really figure out what my stories are about without any barriers or boundaries. It's great to have the bones of my novel done, even if it is only a lousy first draft.

I want to make sure you're hearing me: I'm not suggesting that everyone drop by NaNoWriMo.org and sign up. What I am suggesting is that if you've never given yourself a short deadline or ambitious goals, or you've never surrounded yourself by other encouraging and helpful writers to hold you accountable, it's time to give those methods a try.

For instance, enlist the help of someone close to you, someone you don't want to lose the respect of, and have them give you a deadline and check in with you to ensure you're sticking to it. Or start a Facebook group or Twitter list where you can corral all your writer friends who would like help with accountability. Do you attend a local writing group? If so, why not suggest trying a month of ambitious goal-setting and account-ability among your peers?

Even if the idea of pushing through to write an entire story doesn't appeal to you, I encourage you to set a goal for daily freewriting and observation time to keep your creative juices flowing.

Continued Play

Thomas Edison is quoted as saying, "I have not failed. I have just found ten thousand ways that won't work." Of course, he went on to successfully invent the electric lightbulb, among many other things. Keep a sense of play and positivity as you try out your ideas and follow them through. Don't just half-heartedly try to implement something, and then catalog it as a "bad" or "worthless" idea.

Ten thousand attempts at using each story idea might be overdoing it, but I encourage you to push each of your ideas and make it as extreme as possible. Don't be afraid of your ideas crossing the line of believability. You can always back them off again. If you've never pushed your ideas far enough, you may not yet know how much they could upset your plot or change your characters' lives. To find out where "far enough" is, often you will have to go too far.

In *The Hunger Games*, for example, what if Suzanne Collins had made the challenge for teenagers to fight until one of them was bleeding, rather than fighting to the death? The highest stakes make for exciting and emotionally complex stories.

Or when thinking of stretching and pushing your characters

as far as you can, consider Robin Williams in *Mrs. Doubtfire*. The writer could have simply created a character who gave his all into becoming a responsible adult, demonstrating his capability for caring for his children simply by gaining steady and respectable employment. Instead, the writer pushed this character to become much more interesting — a cross-dressing female nanny who gets to offer his kids the discipline they need part-time, while still remaining their "fun" dad.

In real life there are certain things you just can't say or do, or at least you shouldn't. But in fiction, a man can tell his wife she's fat. Maybe he *should* if your family drama needs a little extra conflict. The conflict that follows might keep the characters and plot exciting, and at the very least, it doesn't hurt to experiment with such directness. Think of all the things you wouldn't say in real life but would like to say. These are all plot ideas you can experiment with.

Most people are afraid to fail, and this fear often limits our creativity. What if we could get past that? Sometimes, failing a few times is all we need to realize it's not the end of the world. As I mention above, push your character and stories until you've pushed too far, past the point of believability. Try and find the line that's "far enough." You can always pull back to recover believability. Unlike real life, "failing" in a story is always fixable and temporary, but it can still feel as scary as real life. If you practice trying things that don't work, or "failing" in your writing, you will be more willing to take creative risks. Often, our stories won't find true success until we are daring enough to risk them failing.

Persevere.

Go with your gut.

And foster creative story ideas every day.

You don't have to write the same thing every day. What are you in the mood for? Polishing your writing? Brainstorming? Freewriting to find a character's voice? Internet research (aka, looking up pictures or places on Google and YouTube)? In-person research?

Whatever you do, do something. Every day, create, brainstorm, and craft your stories. Do that, and you will never be stagnant and lacking ideas, nor will you have trouble following through to the end.

10. Troubleshooting Problems

To swear off making mistakes is easy.
All you have to do is swear off having ideas.

— LEO BURNETT

Desire drives our energy. Ideally, all the brainstorming suggestions in this book will fuel your creativity and give you the energy and desire to write amazing stories using all your new ideas. However, the truth is, sometimes we hit roadblocks while following through. This chapter addresses some of these problems.

If you don't feel like you have it in you to pursue the ideas you've come up with, and your discouragement lasts over weeks or even months, perhaps it's not the right time for this story. If the inner desire is not there, perhaps you're still dealing with *shoulds* instead of *coulds*. And if there really are things you *should* write, how can you quickly complete those projects, so you can move on to the writing of your heart — the projects that seem fun and easy?

The most important thing is not to force yourself to make

every story idea work. If writing becomes a slog, and then stops, put aside what you're doing and go back to brainstorming. Get back to play. The important thing is simply to keep writing and to harness your love for writing in a way that you'll never let it go.

Do You Have Writer's Block?

Claiming to have "writer's block" is taking the easy way out. It treats a lack of productivity as an ailment. Because it's one of those inarguable diagnoses, it acts like a get-out-of-jail-free card. Except, in the end, it is jail. It justifies spending an endless amount of time making zero progress on writing. Writer's block is not usually the inability to write, but rather just a fear of not writing well. Or at least not well enough.

If you struggle with what you consider "writer's block," I encourage you to read the "Be Positive" chapter in part 4. All you really need is a new perspective to overcome it.

Is Your Idea Too Big?

When you think about your story, does it feel overwhelming? Perhaps you're working on a story with multiple narrators and timelines, and suddenly you're doubting your ability to bring it to completion. I've been there. In the last few years, I started working on my first series. As a stand-alone book author, I had no idea how much brainpower was involved in keeping the characters and settings and motives and outcomes straight from book to book! This series started in my mind as three books, and as I continued to brainstorm, it became seven. Yes, a bit overwhelming! But just like when my husband and I decided to renovate our house, or when we decided our yard really needed some landscaping help, I tackled one little piece at a time — trimming the trees, digging the garden, and planting flowers. When it came to my series, I waited for specific days when I felt particularly positive about my progress, or in a strongly focused head space to look at the bigger picture, and little by little, I have almost made it to the end of my series.

I encourage you to try not to let yourself be intimidated by a big project. Break it down into tiny parts if you need to, and only have a look at the bigger picture on days when you feel up to the task. Work on only one aspect at a time, rather than allowing yourself to get inundated by the larger scope. If you are excited about writing a particular scene you've envisioned, but you're not to that point in the story yet, feel free to jump ahead and write it now. Let yourself have fun and feed your excitement while writing. It doesn't have to *all* be work.

Is Your Idea Too Small?

If you feel like you have used up all the ideas for your novel by page fifty, open your brainstorming notebook or files and search for more! This is what my critique partner Rachel Shane does. She looks through her other nearly fully formed ideas to see if she can combine them. I often get well into the writing of a book before I realize I don't have enough ideas to fill three hundred pages. But if you've followed the practices in this book, it should be no problem. Just spend some time and look through your lists of ideas, especially the ones that are almost ready to write. Can you combine this story idea with other ideas? Have you considered each secondary character's needs and wants, their fears and motives, along with your main character's? Perhaps your plot needs a big complication. Maybe you need to expand the cast and the subplots involving your secondary characters. Go back to brainstorming and see where that takes you.

Are You Being a Perfectionist?

Perfectionism equals high standards misdirected. It's great to try to make your shoes match your purse when you're going out or to take an extra thirty seconds to buff the hood of your car on a sunny day, but when making art, especially a *first draft* of art, you don't want to lose the creative energy that births new ideas. Perfectionism can create too much pressure. It can be difficult to see gold nuggets before they're polished, unless you're willing to sort rocks.

Here is my method for when I feel like I'm battling perfectionism: Start before you feel ready. If you wait until all of your ideas are fully formed, you'll be waiting forever. Waiting and doing nothing breeds perfectionism. Move forward with what you have. I think you'll be surprised at how far you can go with it. In her book *Get It Done*, Sam Bennett asks this important question: "How is your desire to do the perfect thing getting in your way of doing anything?"

Do You Have Story Burnout?

What if you choose an idea, and you absolutely love it, but you get a hundred pages into writing your novel, and your idea loses steam? What then?

Oh, if I had a dollar for every time I've asked myself that same question! The truth is, your ideas *will* lose steam, especially if you are working with novel-length fiction. Three hundred (or more) pages is a long time to stay motivated and to believe in your creativity! I haven't worked on a single novel that has not brought me to a point of doubting either the ideas or my ability to bring them to life. Every author I have spoken with has faced this kind of self-doubt as well. I think the key is keeping this apparent steam-loss in perspective.

The first question to ask is: *Why* are you losing steam? Does it truly have to do with your story ideas?

Perhaps, but perhaps not. Maybe when you first conceptualized your idea, it was brilliant and shiny and reflected diamonds and rubies and million-dollar bills from its every surface, but the truth is, any and every idea comes with its own multitude of problems when you actually start to write it as a story. Even if you spend weeks considering the scenarios you may encounter, inevitably, something will not work out as planned or just not "feel right" once you're actually writing.

Maybe you are so immersed in your story, you no longer have a clear perspective on it. For me, this is usually the case. At this point, I have two options: I can put the project aside for a while and work on something else, go for a walk, go grocery shopping, or run errands. Maybe I'll take a couple of weeks away from looking at or even thinking about the project. My other option, and this is the one I usually choose because I am impatient, is this: I keep moving forward, trusting that if I once thought my story ideas had some value, they probably do. I trust that past-Denise is smarter than present-Denise, and if she felt this would make a good story, it probably will. I also put a fair amount of trust in future-Denise, since she's the one who will look at this muddy section where I was obviously confused and not feeling in the groove, and she will be able to come along and fix whatever is wrong. Future-Denise will have a lot more perspective than present-Denise, so I tell present-Denise to simply buckle down, write the first draft, and make it as awful as she wants. It won't matter. The past and future versions of myself are good enough to clean up any literary mess!

Is Your Idea a Dud?

What if your idea is truly a dud? Okay, I won't lie, it *is* possible. Initially, ideas can interest us for all sorts of reasons that don't pan out. Perhaps it's similar to something else we read and loved, but the more we develop our idea, the more we realize we're telling the exact same story, and the original is the *only* way that works with this particular idea.

Maybe the story idea was appealing because it was so completely different than anything else, but delving into it, we realize why no one else has attempted this kind of story before. It's a dud.

Or perhaps the story idea is fraught with unfixable problems (see below), or it doesn't have enough complexity to fill an entire book (see above). Most of the time, there are solutions to whatever the problems are. The first is, if your story is starting to feel like a dud, jump back to the "Fun and Games" section and start brainstorming again. Before you throw out the original idea and call it worthless, at least take some time to play around with it and see if you can unlock some new and exciting possibilities.

Has Your Story Already Been Done?

Has it ever happened that a book comes out that seems to have the exact same premise as the one you're brainstorming or writing? It's happened to me, and most writers I know have had it happen to them. My theory is that ideas float in the atmosphere, and they are fair game for anyone to grab and make use of. Call this a spiritual phenomenon, or a metaphysical one, but it happens too often to be an anomaly. The first lesson here is: Make use of your ideas, or somebody else will!

That said, if you have been diligently developing your idea, and suddenly another book releases with the same premise, please, *please* don't immediately chuck your entire manuscript into the recycle bin! There *is* room in the marketplace for more than one story with a similar premise.

When I was a struggling unpublished writer, I spent about eight years plodding away at a book baby called *Appetite for Beauty*. I loved this book and these characters, and I was very close to the story, as it was born out of my confusion over a good friend's severe eating disorder. The story came from my heart, and so I spent countless hours trying to make it as strong and as polished as it could possibly be.

Fast-forward to the time when I felt this book baby was ready to send out into the world of agents and publishers. I was just perfecting my query letter, when my critique partner sent me a little book announcement blurb from *Publisher's Weekly*.

The book's main character captured the world around her through photography, like mine. The story included an older sister with a severe eating disorder, like mine. It was written for the (still somewhat small) young adult market, also like mine. My critique partner asked if this author had ever read an early version of my book — that's how similar the premise looked to her!

Like me, this author was also unpublished, but unlike me, she already had an agent and editor who had fallen in love with her book. Oh, and did I mention she was a soap opera star, just dipping her toe into writing to give it a try? So this lady had a huge fan base and platform, and a book just like mine that she had already sold. What was I to do?

Well, I may have thrown a few things. I may have had a few drinks. I definitely buried that manuscript deep in my hard drive so it wouldn't cause me to ugly-cry my eyes out every single day.

And I started working on something else.

Fast-forward a few years later, when I had published my first book — the unrelated young adult novel *Losing Faith*. During the long publishing process, I was emotionally bolstered by my success, and I pulled out *Appetite for Beauty* to have another look. I still loved the book, but yet again, I noticed another recent release of a young adult eating disorder–themed book: *Wintergirls* by acclaimed author Laurie Halse Anderson — with writing so haltingly beautiful it took my breath away. I put my manuscript away, since I didn't have much confidence in my poor little book ever seeing the light of day.

Fast-forward again to when my editor for *Losing Faith* asked if I had anything else. Without much hope, I sent *Appetite for*

Beauty to my agent, who forwarded it to my editor, and to my pleasant surprise, she said she was interested in publishing it! You can now find this book on the bookstore shelves under the title *Never Enough*.

Yes, it can be heartbreaking to feel like your idea has been "taken," but I hope my story gives you hope. Maybe it's not too late. Maybe it simply isn't this book's time.

Has someone already written your story idea? Great! Write that same premise, but differently, and by the time yours is written and polished, the market may be ready for a new take. Almost every writer I have ever had an extended conversation with has told me about a great idea that they gave up on because they saw a book just like it on the shelf, on the *New York Times'* list, or in *Publisher's Weekly*. But it doesn't have to be that way.

Yes, every idea under the sun has been written, but nothing is truly finished. There is always a new spin you can put on things, or a new combination of ideas. What about adding a new outlook or setting to an old idea? There is always a way to make an already-written premise feel fresh.

Does the Story Have Unfixable Problems?

With Google, everyone can figure out almost anything these days. Knowledge is at our fingertips. But rather than focus on researching all of the solutions, and possibly feeling like you can't find them quickly enough, focus on asking the right questions. Don't be afraid of things you still question in your story ideas. Remember when it was okay not to know? Before the internet could answer every question?

We live in an age of easy answers, which can make us feel

like we always have to have the correct answers all the time. But that doesn't work in writing fiction. In fiction, sometimes it's only by working through your ideas and actually writing them that you will find your best solutions.

If you've tried writing through to find a solution and haven't been able to, try to put your unfixable problem into words. Pinpoint the problem. Is there no way out for your character? Upon further research, have you learned that the facts of your ideas don't add up? Then investigate the problem from all angles. Interview an expert. Try to state it in three different ways and tell someone else about your problem. Sometimes simply the act of speaking a problem out loud will cause the correct solution to come to us. Give the problem to someone else and ask them to find a solution. Brainstorm a solution with a group of other writers or friends. Reread chapter 3, "Allies."

Maybe your idea doesn't feel exciting or fresh enough. Try setting your story in a new setting. What if your characters were in a bowling alley in Spain? (Do they have bowling alleys in Spain?) Does that open up new possibilities for your characters and plot? Think outside the box for your solutions, especially when you have complicated problems. Try introducing a new ally or opponent to the problem. What if Oprah was dealing with this problem? Or what if Kim Kardashian showed up in your story right now? How would things change? How does adding or changing an element open your mind to new ideas?

If all else fails and you are attached to your story, forget about the problems, at least for the time being, and move on. Keep writing your story. You'd be surprised at how many problems can fix themselves by the end of a draft.

Part IV

S.P.A.R.K. Habits

The unfortunate thing about this world is that good
habits are so much easier to get out of than bad ones.
— W. SOMERSET MAUGHAM

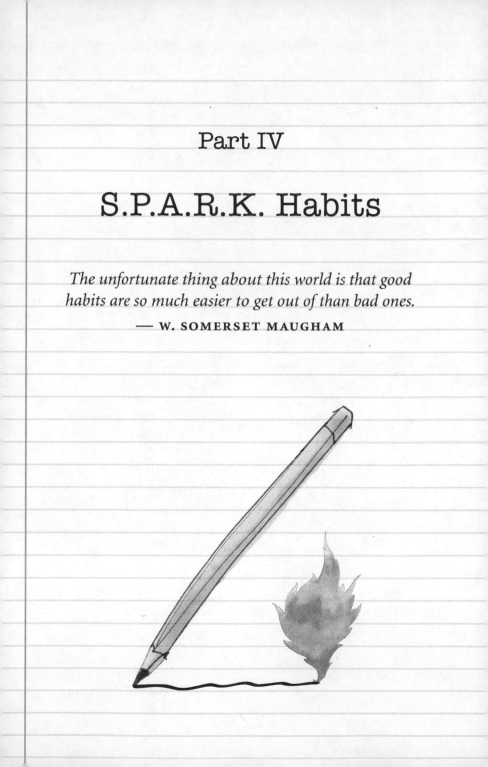

Creating daily and weekly brainstorming habits can prepare you for inspiration. Carry a notebook, or download an app to your phone or tablet that you always carry with you. If you're on an iPhone, I recommend the free app called "A Novel Idea." I have an Android phone and have Google Keep (which is also free) set up for my brainstorming ideas.

Of course, you don't have to be a techno-wizard to be a good brainstormer. Carry a pad of sticky notes, if this is what suits you. Just make sure to bring them all home once you've written on them and add them all to a book or a board on the wall — somewhere central where you can accumulate *all* of your ideas.

Regularly look over what you have accumulated. Play with putting ideas together like puzzle pieces. Find a system that works for you — whether you use spreadsheets or colored Sharpies, find some way of organizing your ideas that is exciting and fun.

This section focuses in detail on how to organize your ideas and on the daily and weekly habits that will keep ideas flowing.

11. Get Organized

Art is the triumph over chaos.

— JOHN CHEEVER

In my book *Fast Fiction,* I talk about my two main brainstorming rules: Basically, that you can never have enough ideas, and that you must keep them organized all in one place. I have gotten so many follow-up questions and comments on these rules, it inspired the book you hold in your hands!

As you gather ideas through brainstorming, you need to stay organized. I organize all of my story ideas into four categories. I prefer to use Google Keep on my phone, which lets you set up a file about absolutely any subject, and then add a title and some notes. You can even add photos, drawings, or recordings to each file. My system is very simple. I have titled four different files: "Characters," "Settings," "Motives," and "Obstacles."

When I come up with a new idea, whether I'm at the grocery store or at one of my son's judo tournaments, I simply open Google Keep, click on the appropriate file, and add any info I've come up with. If I'm at a location that I might want to use as inspiration for a setting, I snap a picture and put it into the "Settings" file of Google Keep.

You absolutely can organize your ideas using the old-fashioned paper-and-pen method, and if you prefer to divide your categories further, such as into "Protagonists," "Antagonists," and "Secondary Characters," feel free. One advantage a technological system may have is the search function, which may be useful once you accumulate lots of ideas. Then again, hard copies of ideas may be more visual and stimulating, so even if you do accumulate your ideas on a phone or a tablet, consider printing them out and pasting them somewhere central and visual at home.

Again, organization does not have to be complicated. Pick up a poster board from a dollar store and draw a line vertically down the middle, and another line horizontally across the middle. Bam! You have a perfect place where all of your fantastic new character, setting, motive, and obstacle ideas can congregate!

12. Find Balance

My point is, life is about balance. The good and the bad.
The highs and the lows. The pina and the colada.

— ELLEN DEGENERES

In all areas, I believe balance is key to living a peaceful and successful life. As the saying goes, "All work and no play" makes for a dull life. But what about all creativity and no responsibility? Even if that were a possibility, I'd like to argue that this would not make anyone happy.

You see, daydreaming and creating are important, yes, but without a strong left brain to come along and order those thoughts and make intelligent decisions, an all-creative person may be left with a pile of useless "art" that no one else wants or is able to see.

Some argue that you can be smart *or* artsy, driven *or* creative, head-led *or* heart-led, but I say you can and should strive to be a mix of all these things. Everyone has a measure of creativity in them — whether or not they foster it is what makes the difference. Everyone has smarts and drive and a responsible side, but some ignore those parts of themselves, while others value and practice them.

I say embrace and grow all sides of your brain! Spend time daydreaming and brainstorming ideas each day, but also spend time scheduling yourself and your writing and organizing your notes. Spend some time focusing on the nonartsy areas of your life, thereby giving your artistic side a much-needed nap. When you come back to being creative again, your juices will be eager to flow, rather than tired and in need of replenishing.

The truth is, the well of creativity can certainly grow by using it. All areas of the brain grow with use and practice, just like any muscle. But creativity will also grow when you give it a rest, take the pressure off, and realign your focus for a while.

There are good reasons for a writer to keep his or her day job, and not only for income. Sometimes the mere task of having another thing you *have to* focus on for a while will give your story-making creative brain the break it needs. Plus, your creative side may thrive better if you aren't relying on writing for your income. Your creative side really doesn't need the kind of pressure that comes with grocery bills and mortgage payments.

It's the conundrum of current-day society. Yes, we respect artists through the ages, we value them and their contributions to society, but our society does not make it easy to make a living as an artist. Artists are on their own, for the most part, needing to perform, perform, perform in order to make even a meager income from their craft. It's too much pressure for the creative brain. Even if your hope is to make a living from your art, I encourage you to keep thinking of it as a hobby for your art's sake. Relax your creative mind at every turn to avoid creative burnout.

On the other hand, if writing is your "business," or you want it to be, I encourage you to spend some time honing your business skills as well as your artistic ones. If you hire out the business work, take up another artistic form as a hobby. You see, the creative brain, in order to thrive, also needs opportunity for creative playtime — a time without anything at stake, and we all know that businesses have plenty at stake.

What does balance look like in practice? Whenever your story ideas start to feel flat or incomplete, take a break and do your taxes. Or paint a painting. Or turn on some music and spin a few pirouettes.

13. Be Positive

Believing a matter to be easy,
it becomes so for you.

— ÉMILE COUÉ

In **The Happiness Project,** Gretchen Rubin suggests we shouldn't be afraid to use our best ideas. It may be our tendency to want to save them, but instead we should trust we will get more and better ideas. Rubin says, "Spending out, to become rich."

I admit, thinking and acting and speaking positive words takes practice. My husband and I went to a success-building seminar with T. Harv Eker several years ago. One of his little tricks for positivity was to thank the universe for any money that came his way — even if it was only a penny he saw lying on the sidewalk. I can still hear Eker's words every time I see a bit of change lying around. "I am a money magnet. Thank you, thank you, thank you!"

This may seem extreme, but in this world where gunmen

are walking into our schools and our nightclubs, I think it takes some extreme measures to foster an ongoing positive attitude.

The truth is, you are more likely to take action when you're feeling hopeful than hopeless, and who wants to feel hopeless, anyway, even if there may be good reasons for it in our world? There is a connection between positivity and creativity because, if you don't believe anything good and beautiful and valuable is going to come from your art, why would you work at it?

Another trick I learned from a friend of mine, when some fact or memory eludes me, is never to say, "I can't remember." Instead, he told me to say, "It'll come to me." Or "I will figure this out." I regularly apply this to my writing, and surprisingly, it always works.

Start here: Believe you will come up with the ideas and answers you are looking for. Say this out loud. Then harness everything that comes into your path. Speak out new ideas to process them in more than one way. Start your idea with "what if" and speak with excitement in your voice as you say it. Try seeing your new idea in a positive light and see what happens.

I find that faith-filled thinking works better than logical or rational thinking when it comes to creativity. No matter how great you feel your ideas are, a time will come when you will likely second-guess them. Practice suspending your disbelief, in the same way you want readers to do when reading your fiction. Push past your self-doubt and say out loud, "I'm having faith right now that this is a great idea." In the end, pushing past your doubts and working fully through your ideas is the only way you'll really know if they are viable.

Sure, failure is a possibility, but that keeps the tension high and creates excitement. This excitement and tension will leak into your writing, and it reminds me of the tightrope walker Philippe Petit, who walked a tightrope between the Twin Towers in New York in 1974 (which was dramatized in the movie *The Walk*). Petit saw the tension and possibility of failure while walking a tightrope as an analogy for life. Anything less than that is not really living! Try thinking of your own process of writing in this same light. Be willing to take creative chances.

Always take notice of what is working, and not only of what is not. I have some fantastic critique partners whom I implore to be hypercritical of my work. I'd rather know from them ahead of time what's not working in my stories than from readers once my books hit the shelves. But I always also ask my critique partners what works best in my stories. When you're working through multiple revisions on a story you've put your heart into, self-doubt will likely hit you often. This is no time to be humble; ask people to point out the positive attributes of your work. You want to give your stories and ideas a fair shake. They say that when we hear something critical about ourselves, it takes ten positive attributes to make up for it, since we play the negative comment over in our minds again and again. Doesn't this apply to our stories and ideas as well? Ask for the positive, and force your own mind to dwell there as often as you can.

Recognize and be thankful for the good ideas you've had in the past. If you're constantly running the inner mantra, "I can never come up with good ideas," guess what. You won't be able to. What you focus on grows. So focus on the areas where you have had success in the past. Your inner dialogue about the past *will* affect how well you mine ideas in the future. Remember the *Little Engine That Could*? Think you can, think you can, and you can! All self-talk, everything that rolls through your mind, affects your self-image and therefore your performance. Believe that you already have lots of ideas, and guess what. You will.

Worry can also kill your ideas before they've been given a chance to fully develop. "Trying to relax" about something you're concerned about doesn't usually work. Instead, schedule your brainstorming/idea-mining time for when you're in the midst of another low-mental activity. I get some of my best ideas while driving, for instance. While your brain is partially focused on something else, it takes the pressure off and can help you relax as you seek new ideas. Thankfully, I have a job and family that require me to be on the road a lot, so it helps me to corral a lot of ideas. (Now, if only I had enough time to write them all!)

If you tend toward a negative outlook, try my husband's method for fostering positivity. Each night before bed, my husband jots three new things into his "Success" or "Gratitude" journal — including anything from the day that was a positive accomplishment or experience for him. Filmmaker Roko Belic says, "Gratitude is a shortcut to happiness," so why not try to foster your gratitude for what is going well in your life? And trust me, there is always *something* to be thankful for. Are you able to read this book? Great, you're more fortunate than the 758 million adults around the world who are illiterate. There is always someone worse off than you. It's fine to start with gratefulness for the small things, like that you remembered to buy cream for your coffee. That's okay! Soon you'll be noticing good fortune everywhere in your life.

If you tend to focus on the negative, think of it this way: Even *that* can be a good thing when it comes to story ideas. Storytellers are ultimately problem solvers. It doesn't hurt to notice real-life problems and wonder, "What is the solution?" Or even, "What if it was worse?" Don't be afraid of problems and hurdles and obstacles. Harness them, and get better and better at coming up with creative solutions.

What if you started today with what you already have and knew it would become something great? What if you could not fail? What if you could simply suspend your disbelief for a short time about the possibility of failure? Would it make a difference to your writing?

In the end, I encourage you to treat every single idea as viable and valuable; try to expand on each one and assess how or where you might use it. Pretend the *New York Times* has phoned and told you they've gotten wind of your next story idea, and it's sure to sell a million copies. Imagine this happening with every single idea you have. Does it change how hard you're willing to work? Does it change your excitement? Develop your ideas with confidence, trusting that you will find brilliance if you put your time into them.

Maybe this one *is* a great idea, a revolutionary one. How will you ever know unless you give it the benefit of the doubt?

14. Get Active

Physical fitness is not only one of the most important keys to a healthy body; it is the basis of dynamic and creative intellectual activity.
— JOHN F. KENNEDY

I know you've heard it a million times: Work out, get fit, look after your body. You've likely heard a lot of different reasons to become more active — everything from preventing heart disease to affecting hormones. But I'm not here to encourage you to get in shape. In fact, don't even do anything outside your comfort zone. Don't train hard or give it your all. You heard me exactly right.

Rather, to boost your creative powers, I suggest mild, mindless activity. Go for a walk around the block. Get up out of your office chair and do some knee bends. Pace from your kitchen to your bedroom and back. Swing your arms in figure-eight formations until it's mindless. Just get moving.

Here's a new formula:

Daily Creativity + Daily Activity = Health, Joy, and Happiness

A 2013 report in the *Telegraph News* discussed how daily physical activity boosts cognitive creativity. Exercising regularly four times per week or more has been shown to improve our creative ability to come up with solutions.

There is a valid reason why writers often drop everything and go for a walk. The circulation created by a short walk gets things moving in the brain as well as the body. The more your ideas flow, the more at peace you will be while creating. Thus, my formula above.

"Physical activity gets your mind into the bodily experience, so that subconscious connections can pop up," says Keith Sawyer, an associate professor in the Department of Education at Washington University in St. Louis. "If you take breaks — what I call 'idle time,' ideally spent in solitary activities, such as walking, running, or biking — your mind frees up to cross-fertilize so that when you return to intellectual pursuits, you're far better at connecting ideas that at first glance don't seem to be obvious or even related."

Set your mind on something else for a short time. Allow your brain to relax from the problem at hand. Relaxing the brain will allow the superior temporal gyrus, the part of the brain responsible for solving problems, to kick in and offer insight. Tensely focusing without rest doesn't allow this part of the brain to work as efficiently.

When you work out, your body flushes out the stress hormone cortisol, relieving your brain function for creativity and problem solving, rather than constantly working hard at relieving your stress.

In *The Creative Habit: Learn It and Use It for Life*, legendary choreographer Twyla Tharp details Beethoven's creative habit: "Although he was not physically fit, Beethoven would start each day with the same ritual: a morning walk during which he would scribble into a pocket sketchbook the first rough notes of whatever musical idea inevitably entered his head. Having done that, having limbered up his mind and transported himself into his version of a trance zone during the walk, he would return to his room and get to work."

A 2005 report in *Creative Research Journal* suggests that creative potential is increased for up to two hours after moderate exercise. Thus, although it's great if you can write immediately after a workout or a walk, you have at least a two-hour window of enhanced creativity. Even better, be prepared to take down ideas as they arise *while* exercising. According to studies, long-term consistent exercise proves more valuable to creative brain function than a singular occurrence of exercise.

So don't go hard or excessively long. Just go regularly. Just get moving.

If you're like me, ideas will rarely show up when you're sitting at your desk waiting for them. Switch gears when you need to do a little brainstorming. Go for a walk or a bike ride. Do something to take the pressure off of your creative mind, and you'll be surprised how quickly your creativity kicks in.

Likewise, frustration rarely leads to great ideas. If the particular story you're working on is not coming together or is missing something you can't seem to pinpoint, give this one a rest. Work on something else for a while, at least until it feels like the pressure has lifted.

If all else fails, walk it out.

15. Rest

There must be quite a few things a hot bath won't cure,
but I don't know many of them.

— SYLVIA PLATH

Many writers tout a greater ability to be creative first thing in the morning, so why not give it a try? Not to mention, spending a few minutes brainstorming first thing in the day automatically makes it a priority in your life. Once you're off to your busy daily responsibilities, isn't it likely this pursuit might get passed by or forgotten?

Another consideration is hours slept. Getting eight to nine hours of deep sleep per night reduces the stress hormone cortisol in the body, allowing the brain to focus on being creative. Make getting enough sleep at night a priority, and you'll notice you're automatically making your creative brain a priority. It will thrive in the daytime as well, when it has had enough time to play in your dreams.

Let's talk about your waking moments. Do you tend to get so closely focused on your creative work that you find you get stressed out about it? That stress will not go away from simply focusing harder. In fact, it will probably have the opposite effect.

Think of something else for a while. Go grocery shopping, take a shower, or enjoy a hot bath. Let the mind rest and turn things over at its leisure without any push. Sleep on it. Do simple tasks that will allow your mind to wander. Something as seemingly unfruitful as taking a nap may be the thing that solves your writer's block. Perhaps you'll wake with the perfect solution. Sometimes we have to stop trying too hard. Laugh — it's a release for your brain. And as Jack Foster tells us in his book *How to Get Ideas*, it is difficult to have humor without creativity. Take a moment to recall the funniest person you know. Find something to laugh at, and your mind will relax and be ready to get back to your creative work in no time.

16. Constantly Change

Progress is impossible without change,
and those who cannot change their minds
cannot change anything.

— GEORGE BERNARD SHAW

I suggest changing your daily routine in absolutely any way you can to help you see the world from a different perspective. Lie on the floor in your living room for a few minutes, doing nothing but looking around. Choose a different bathroom stall at the office. Go to a different grocery store the next time you have to pick up a few things. Take a different route to work.

Changing your routine whenever possible reminds you to be observant. You won't just skip by all the details you've seen again and again.

You can change in other ways, too, that will likely spark new observations in your life. Diversify your social circle. Spend more time with a grandparent or child, someone who has lived in a different generation, or someone who has lived in a different country.

Change creative pursuits. Go cook something elaborate in the kitchen. Dance. Try your hand at martial arts. Paint. Draw. Carve. Create a fun hopscotch on the sidewalk in front of your house.

Do things differently in any way you can. Sit in a different chair than you normally sit and see how the vantage point changes. Put your clothes on in a different order. Take the scenic route when you have time. Read something out of your normal reading genre. If you're used to novels, read a magazine or a book of poetry. Watch different genres of TV shows or movies. If you usually watch crime dramas, try a comedy or a documentary. Order something unusual at a restaurant. Take an unusual seminar, workshop, or class. Listen to a different kind of music, and then get up and dance to it. Give yourself a wide variety of experience to draw from to help open your mind and lift any creative barriers you may unknowingly put on yourself.

Commit to one hour per day of observing, learning, or reading something different. Set aside one of those hours each week for exploratory Google time. Do a Google search on subjects that interest you but which you've never pursued. Look for new subjects that could be interesting. Learn new facts so you can hold an intelligent conversation on a new subject, and then find someone to intelligently converse with.

Set aside a daily time for deliberate learning. If you *had* to learn about a new subject, what would it be? Your best and most inspired learning will be diverse, spanning a wide variety of subject matters that truly interest you.

17. Weekly S.P.A.R.K. Habits

Writers are completely out of touch with reality.
Writers are a crazy person. We create conflict — for a living.
We do this all the time, sometimes on a weekly basis;
we create horrible, incredible circumstances and then
figure a way out of them. That's what we do.

— JOSS WHEDON

This section has so far focused on daily habits you can implement right away and anytime, such as going for a walk or changing routines to spark your observation muscles. These things don't take much time, and they are good for your health and to keep your mind young and agile.

This chapter gathers a few suggestions I have for weekly or more occasional activities. They would be difficult for most people to do daily because they take a little more time and focused energy. Give them a try. If they work to inspire your creativity, I encourage you to make them a regular weekly habit. You don't have to do all of these every week, and you can certainly stick to only one if you have a favorite. But encourage your mind to play and have fun with your ideas every single week. Teach your creative mind through practice and repetition that it is allowed to try new things, even if they might not grow into anything serious in the end. (But you never know...they might!)

As with all the brainstorming ideas in this book, once you have rewritten, expanded, or played with the ideas, file them away under the appropriate categories. This will help you remember them when you need them most. Who knows, you may feel so inspired, one simple idea could turn into an entire book!

Dream On

Your brain isn't sleeping when you are. Rather, it enters a new, creative state of consciousness: dreams.

Have you ever woken up with the remnants of a dream playing out in your subconscious? What do you notice about these dreams? I'll bet they are not normally the type of scenes and situations you'd think up during your daytime conscious state. Perhaps they have strange or misplaced architecture. Maybe they bring people together who would never meet in real life, or they include a talking animal or an impossible feat.

Dreams and your sleep state release a whole new realm of ideas. Use them to fill your arsenal. Yes, some will be crazy "pizza dreams," which arise only from an abundance of heavy foods the night before, and they may contain ideas that are too extreme to work in either real life or fiction. But some dreams will shed new light on people, places, and situations. Some may infuse you with the emotional energy you need for a particular character or story. Some may just be plain old creative ideas that your brain was too busy and distracted to conceive of during the day.

This postdream waking state is called sleep inertia or the hypnopompic state. I recommend keeping a notebook beside your bed and jotting down notes upon waking — anything at all you can remember from your dream state. You can always cross out these ideas later, if your conscious brain decides they are no good, the result of a surplus of pepperoni and cheese. But at least write them down. I recommend doing this before you speak to another person (or animal) if at all possible. Once you start speaking, you start processing in a more logical and less open-minded or creative way.

Then, once a week, look through your dream journal to compare, combine, and circle your favorite dreamed-up ideas.

Fun Friday!

Keep a weekly log of ideas. At the end of the week, before you file these away in their respective categories — such as characters, settings, motives, and obstacles — pick three of your favorites. I do this every Friday and refer to it as *Fun Friday*. It usually only takes five minutes to skim over my ideas from the week and pick three, and then I spend another ten minutes or so with one or more of the exercises below.

Idea Map

Take one of your three favorite ideas from the week, and spend a few minutes making an idea map with one of them (see page 53). If one of your ideas is "A lakeshore cabin in the dreary dead of winter," write that in the middle of a blank page. Draw maybe ten or fifteen lines outward from the phrase, and at each line's end write down anything at all that comes to mind regarding this cabin. This can include inhabitants, weather, building descriptions, a history of the cabin — anything at all!

If you want, do this with all three ideas. These explorations do not have to relate at all with one another.

Freewrite

Write one idea at the top of a blank page, and freewrite for five minutes, telling a quick, off-the-cuff, no-pressure story. Say, if your idea was "a middle-age man named Albert," then you'd describe one event in Albert's life. Describe the setting for the scene, and consider what other characters might be part of Albert's life. What goal might drive him? Every once in a while, it's a good idea to do some creative writing that carries no pressure to give your creative mind a sense of free play.

Bob the Bold Interview

My fictional friend Bob loves to ask point-blank questions for his famous (and also fictional) radio show — *The Best Ideas Ever!* Play along with Bob and be interviewed about one of your favorite ideas. Either write your answers on paper or record them with your phone app, which gives you that live-radio feel. Here are Bob's most popular questions, but feel free to add some of your own!

Bob: Where on earth did you get such a spectacular idea?

Your answer: _____

Bob: Wow, interesting! Now, I know you're in the early stages of development with this idea, but can you give us any hints of where you plan to go with it?

Your answer: _____

Bob: That sounds exciting! I heard a rumor that [insert name of best-selling author in the same genre] has been toying with the same idea. If he/she goes forward with it, what kind of story do you think he/she would come up with?

Your answer: _____

Bob: Sure, right. But I like your plan much better. Now help our listeners understand the kind of intense conflict that could arise from an idea like this one.

Your answer: _____

Bob: Oooh, I'm getting chills! And what do you love most about this idea?

Your answer: _____

Bob: Thank you so much for being here, Awesome Writer! Now before you go off and become famous, I'd better grab your autograph.

Conclusion

I can't tell you the number of people I have talked to who rattle off what seems to be an endless stream of story ideas they think *I* should write. I can't call these people writers (though I'd like to). The problem is that they don't do anything with these ideas except rattle them off and then wait for someone else to implement them. They may be professional brainstormers, but they are not writers because they do not sit down to do the actual writing. What good is the best idea in the world if it never gets developed?

Now that you have some ideas to start with, go sit in one of your favorite coffee shops and enjoy a caramel macchiato while brainstorming how to best implement them. Or go attend an opera if your idea is opera-based. Attend a baseball game or the theater or an amusement park if it will help inspire your story. Sometimes it's important for us to shell out a few dollars to remind ourselves there is value in bringing our unique stories to fruition.

Don't be the person who talks about all their great ideas at a cocktail party, and then ten years later has never done anything with them. If you need help, there are plenty of great writing guides that take you through the planning of a novel. I recommend my book *Fast Fiction*, but there are many others out there, too.

When it comes to plotting out novel-length works, I encourage you to try the software Scrivener. This program makes it easy to divide your ideas into separate notes and files, and it makes it easy to take chances. I wrote this entire book in Scrivener. Scrivener makes it easy to move sections of text around, save them for later, and file bits away without losing them.

Whatever method of turning your ideas into a finished story excites you, that's what you should use. Just like, whatever idea-mining methods and exercises excite you — those are what you should use.

I hope this book has provided plenty of food for thought about how many great story ideas you already have in your life, right there waiting for you to discover them. I love to hear from readers and how they have implemented my writing advice and what, specifically, has worked for them. Feel free to drop me a line anytime at d@denisejaden.com.

All the best with your future writing projects, and may your sparks turn into an ever-burning flame!

Appendixes

These appendixes provide lists of names and story ideas to help spark your creativity. Their aim is to keep you in a state of forward momentum as you work on creating new stories. They can be used as simply placeholders or as elements you will keep, but they are intended to keep you from getting blocked or jammed up in your creation process.

These appendixes are by no means exhaustive. They are simply references to help launch your mind into a creative mode. Use these ideas as you like, and feel free to modify them at will. Make notes of your own ideas in the margins (so long as this is not a library copy!) and keep building on your ideas as they erupt within you.

Appendix A: Names

For additional character names, including specific ethnicities, I've provided several online name generators in the endnotes. When choosing a cast of names for a story, it is best to vary starting letter/sound, length, and commonality of names to help readers individualize your characters.

Common Female Names

Abigail/Abby/Gail
Aisha
Alice
Amanda
Amy
Angelique/Angela
Ann/Anna/Anne
Arlene
Barbara/Barb
Betty
Brenda

Carissa
Carolyn/Carol/Carrie
Charlotte/Char
Christine/Chrissy/Chris
Cynthia
Dawn
Deborah/Debbie
Desiree
Donna
Dorothy/Dot
Eileen

Elena	Laura/Laurie/Lori
Elisa	Leanne/Lee/Lea
Elizabeth/Liz/Beth	Leila
Ellen	Linda
Emily	Lisa
Fatima	Lucinda
Florence	Lynn
Frances	Margaret/Margie/Peggy
Gabrielle/Gabby	Maria/Marie/Mary
Georgia	Melissa/Mel
Gina	Michelle
Gloria	Min
Grace	Monique
Hazel	Nancy
Heather	Natalie
Helen	Natasha/Tasha
Ida	Nicola/Nicole
Irene	Nina
Isabella/Izzy/Bella	Nora
Jacqueline/Jackie	Norma
Janet	Olive
Jennifer/Jen	Olivia
Jessica/Jessie/Jess	Oni
Josephine/Josie	Pamela/Pam
Juanita	Patricia/Pat
Judith/Judy	Paula
Karen	Penny
Kathleen/Kate/Kat/Kit/Kitty	Phyllis
Kimberly/Kim	Rachel

Rebecca/Becca

Rhonda

Rida

Rosa/Rose

Ruby

Ruth

Salima

Sandra

Sarah/Sara

Sharon

Shirley

Sophia/Sophie

Stephanie

Susan/Sue

Tammy/Tam

Theresa

Tina

Tisa

Tracy

Veronica

Victoria/Vicki

Virginia/Ginny

Vivian/Viv

Wanda

Wendy

Yolanda

Zan

Common Male Names

Albert

Alexander/Alex/Zander

Alfred

Allen/Al

Amir

Andrew/Andy

Angelo

Anthony/Antonio/Tony

Arthur/Art

Benjamin/Ben

Bradley/Brad

Brian

Bruce

Carl

Charles/Chuck

Christopher/Chris

Claude

Curtis

Daniel/Dan/Danny

Dante

David/Dave

Dennis

Diego

Dominic/Dom

Donald/Don

Donovan

Earl	José
Edward/Ed	Joseph/Joe
Eric/Erik	Joshua/Josh
Felix	Kamal
Frank	Kareem
Fred/Freddie	Karl
Gabriel/Gabe	Keith
Gary	Kenneth/Ken
George	Kevin
Gino	Lawrence/Larry
Gregory/Greg	Lee/Li
Guy	Leroy
Harold/Harry	Lorenzo
Harrison	Luis
Hasan	Mark/Marcel/Marco
Hector	Martin
Henry	Matthew/Matt
Howard/Howie	Michael/Mike
Ian	Nathaniel/Nathan/Nate/Nat
Isaac	Nicholas/Nick
Ivan	Norman/Norm
Jack	Oscar
Jamal	Patrick/Pat
James/Jim	Paul
Jason	Peter/Pete
Jeffrey/Jeff	Phillip/Phil
Jerry	Quintin
Jin	Raymond/Ray
Jonathan/John/Jean	Richard/Rick

Robert/Roberto/Bobby/Bob
Ronald/Ron
Salim
Scott
Sebastian
Stephen/Steve
Teddy/Ted
Terry
Thomas/Tommy/Tom
Timothy/Tim
Todd

Travis
Umi
Victor/Vic
Vincent/Vince
Wade
Wallace/Wally
Walter/Walt
Wesley/Wes
William/Bill
Yen
Zachary/Zack

Unusual Female Names

Agate
Aiyana
Alabama
Altair
Alyvia
Arabeth
Ardra
Atlas
Augusta
Aurelia
Aviva
Bentlee
Breena
Brenna
Brielle
Bronwyn

Calypso
Cambria
Caryne
Carys
Cassia
Casspian
Cleo
Cyprian
Dasi
Derris
Destin
Devlyn
Devon
Diem
Dinah
Dorian

Dorothea

Dynie

Eira

Ellison

Errine

Eryke

Esme

Eulalia

Evanth

Farale

Fay

Fenella

Fineas

Finian

Fleur

Gavina

Gavriel

Georgina

Glynna

Greenlee

Griffin

Hannelore

Harmonia

Heavenly/Heaven

Hermione

Honey

Huxley

Iagan

Idalia

Ignacia

Indigo

Indre

Jazz

Jessalyn

Juno/Juneau

Kansas

Karensa

Karran

Katana

Kierst

Kira

Kyale

Kyler

Ladia

Larkyn

Leala

Leonora

Liara

Lilith

Liora

Lulu

Lyrik

Madonna

Maple

Marius

Maylea

Monet

Mora

Moriana	Samia
Moxie	Saskia
Natalia	Sephya
Natania	September
Neveah	Serenity
Nico	Shaundra
Novalie	Siveth
Nyssa	Snow
Octavia	Storm
Olympia	Story
Oralie	Sunshine
Orian	Swayze
Perigrine	Tamsin
Perpetua	Tate
Phelan	Thalia
Pilar	Thana
Primrose	Torian
Psalm	Tristana
Pyralia	Truly
Quintessa	Tulip
Quiss	Uriela
Raisa	Valiah
Remi	Valkyrie
Rhyan	Vanora
Riona	Verity
Rogue	Vesper
Sadi	Vita
Sailor	Xara
Salina	Yadira

Yakira

Zadie

Zaira

Zane

Zelda

Zi

Zinnia

Zora

Zowie

Unusual Male Names

Achard

Aerden

Alaric

Alaron

Alynd

Apollo

Aristotle

Arrow

Asgoth

Auden

Aurelio

Baker

Berryn

Biston

Blade

Blaise/Blaze

Bolrock

Bowie

Bram

Brax

Casden

Casimir

Caspian

Cater

Cedar

Chamon

Chap

Chet

Constantine

Cordale

Cosmo

Daburn

Derrib

Dex

Drophar

Elthin

Eryk

Everest

Evo

Fausto

Fenrir

Ferris

Fischer

Fitzgerald

Floran/Florian	Lan
Fulton	Larson
Gavin	Laszlo
Geth	Ledo
Gorth	Lev
Gryffin	Lor
Halmar	Macon
Hanes	Maguire
Hart	Mavel
Hawk	Mercer
Hectar	Milandro
Heston	Nadeer
Hyten	Nile
Iarmod	Niro
Ikar	Nythil
Illium	Ocarin
Inigo	Occhi
Jager	Octavius
Jansen	Oden
Janus	Ospar
Jarak	Ozias
Jasek	Padan
Jedi	Pascal
Jex	Pax
Kael	Penn
Kafar	Perder
Keran	Peregrine
Kurn	Phoenix
Laird	Pi

Poet
Quest
Quid
Quipar
Rafferty
Raith
Reapar
Rio
Rockwell
Rykar
Sandar
Scout
Sharn
Shaw
Shepherd
Silko
Skylar
Slater
Stellan
Tarran
Teo
Thane
Topaz
Tor
Torc

Travys
Trebor
True
Tylien
Undin
Uther
Vaccon
Vicart
Voltaine
Werner
Weshin
West
Whit
Wrathran
Xander
Xaviear
Xex
Yabaro
Yessirn
Zak
Zayn
Zeren
Zeus
Zircon

Popular Surnames

Adams
Ali
Allen

Anderson
Aslan
Baker

Brown	Jang
Campbell	Johnson
Carter	Jones
Clark	Kane
Collins	Kent
Cortez	Khan
Davis	Kimura
Dawson	King
Delacruz	Kwon
Edwards	Lam
Eng	Lee
Evans	Lewis
Fisher	Lin
Fitzgerald	Lopez
Fong	Martin
Fox	Martinez
Garcia	Miller
Gomez	Mitchell
Gonzalez	Molina
Green	Moore
Hall	Nelson
Han	Newton
Harris	Nicholson
Hasan	O'Connor
Hernandez	Olsen
Hill	Owen
Ingram	Parker
Irving	Perez
Isaac	Phillips
Jackson	Quigley

Quinn

Roberts

Robinson

Rodriguez

Scott

Sharma

Smith

Spencer

Tam

Taylor

Thomas

Thomson

Turner

Unsworth

Upton

Vale

Vickers

Vincent

Yates

York

Yoshida

Young

Walker

White

Williams

Wilson

Wright

Appendix B: Places

If you fall into the habit of using the same old settings
— either the same ones in your own stories or the same ones
you've read about in a thousand books — then use this appendix for "sparks" to find new places for your characters.

Remember, each setting suggests types of actions, and each
has its own sights, sounds, and smells. How might your story
idea unfold or feel differently in one of these settings?

Airplane	Bus station
Airplane hangar	Cabin
Airport	Café
Alley	Casino
Apartment	Cathedral
Arcade	Cave
Army base	Chapel
Art studio	Church
Auto shop	Clubhouse
Bar	College
Beach	Concert hall
Bowling alley	Cruise ship
Bus	Dance studio

Darkroom

Dentist's office

Doctor's office

Drugstore

Farm

FBI headquarters

Fitness center

Forest

Garage

Greenhouse

Grocery store

Gymnasium

Gymnastics studio

Hair salon

Helicopter

Hospital

Hunting cabin

Ice arena

Igloo

Institution

Jail

Lakeside

Laser tag arena

Library

Loft

Martial arts dojo

Masquerade ball

Mill

Monument

Movie theater

Nightclub

Nursery

Nursing home

Park

Pier

Police station

Pool hall

Post office

Preschool

Pub

Public restroom

Ranch

Resort

Salesroom

School

Senior center

Shoe store

Shopping mall

Spa

Spaceship

Space station

Swimming pool

Theater

Theme park

Thrift store

Train

Train station

Tunnel

University

Upscale neighborhood

Warehouse

Zoo

Appendix C: Motives

Motive can be the most complicated element when fleshing out your story ideas. Often characters are unaware of their own motives, or motives are too complex for even your character to understand. You may find that a different motive emerges during the actual writing of your story than the one you had planned on.

But every engaging character in every good story needs a motive, a kick in the pants, or the key that unlocks their intentions, and this list can help you brainstorm this element. These motives are generalized, but you can adapt them to your specific story in any number of different ways.

Acceptance, or fitting in

Acknowledgment

Atonement

Beauty

Being wrongfully accused

Defending home, school, or
    business

Doing the right thing

Dream job

Dream vacation

Drugs

Emulating others

Escaping danger, fears, or self

Excellence, or being the best

Exoneration

Failure avoidance

Family or marital conflict

Family or marital loyalty

Family tradition
Following the rules
Freedom
Friendship
Fulfilling a collection
Fulfilling or disproving
    destiny
Glory
Greed
Happiness
Honor
Ideals or idealism
Immortality
Indebtedness
Inspirational dream
Integrity
Jealousy
Justice
Keeping a secret
Love
Loyalty
Manliness
Materialism
Meeting a challenge
Money
Moral virtue
Motherhood
Normalcy

Obeying the law
Overcoming obstacle or
    bad guys
Overcoming self, fear, or
    weakness
Passing an exam or test
Patriotism
Physical improvement
Popularity
Property dispute
Prophecy
Protecting a vulnerable
    person or animal
Quest for understanding
    or help
Rebellion
Recovering what's lost
Religious beliefs
Repayment
Rescuing loved one
Resolution
Restitution
Returning or going home
Revenge
Romance
Saving the world
Scientific discovery
Seeking purpose

Self-preservation

Sex

Significance

Specialness

Strength

Survivor guilt

Tragic dream

Vanity

Vindication

Vow

Winning

Youth

Appendix D: Obstacles

As it is in life, our fictional characters face many obstacles. Ultimately, obstacles in your story should feel intrinsic to the plot and the characters, but in the spirit of brainstorming, throw a giant rock at your characters, Indiana Jones style, and see what happens! Obstacles should surprise both characters and readers and involve high stakes. Make obstacles as dire as possible, so characters seem strong and larger than life when they overcome them. Here is a sampling of obstacles, which are grouped by the basic scenario they represent.

Person vs. Person

Abusive parent

Angry teacher

Communication lapse

Demanding parent

Greedy boss

Jealous spouse

Kidnapper

Marital conflict

Prison warden

Skilled competitor

Terrorist

Unethical doctor

Person vs. Nature

Angelic or spiritual
    interference
Asteroid
Being lost
Being trapped
Difficult climate
Disease outbreak
Earthquake
Fire
Flood
Guard dog

Hurricane
Impossible quest
Monsters
Rough terrain to navigate
Shipwreck
Storm
Supernatural occurrence
Tornado
Tsunami
Wild animal
Zombies

Person vs. Society

Chauvinism
Dictatorship
Fitting in
Incarceration
Old way of thinking
Political beliefs

Protest
Racism
Religious beliefs
Rules
Segregation
Traditions

Person vs. Self

Physical Limitations:
Amputated limb
Blindness
Deafness
Illness

Muteness or inability to
    communicate
Physical weakness
Stutter
Wounding

Mental Limitations:

Addiction
Inexperience
Lack of perspective
Lack of smarts
Lack of specific knowledge

Lack of technological
  expertise
Rash decisions or behaviors
Wrong or misinterpreted
  teaching

Emotional Limitations:

Anger
Confusion
Delusions
Emotional or psychiatric
  disorder
Heartache

Lack of drive or
  motivation
Rage
Sadness
Unbridled drive or
  motivation

Appendix E: Story Themes

Capturing and breaking down themes can be an arguable topic. Some would say all stories basically boil down to ten or twenty themes, while others say there are hundreds of story themes. Here is a list of themes to help with brainstorming.

Abandonment vs. belonging

Acceptance of true self or
abilities and limitations

Accepting others for who
they are

Accepting the past or a
possible future

Accepting the world as it is

Belief in self leads to
fulfillment

Bravery pays off or shows
inner strength

Change vs. tradition

Coming of age is common
to all

Community vs. isolation

Dangers of ignorance

Death brings new life, or the
circle of life

Dreams vs. reality

Drive can overcome any
obstacle

Duty vs. calling

Escape vs. staying power

Faith in friends or family gets
you through

Faith or spirituality gets you
through

Faith that the world is
inherently good

Family is a blessing or a curse

Fate vs. free will

Forgive and be forgiven

Forgiveness frees the forgiver

Give selflessly and it will
    come back to you

Good conquers all

Greed vs. generosity

Hard work pays off

Heart overcomes all obstacles

Inner strength vs. outer
    strength

Intolerance leads to downfall

Isolation vs. trusting others

Knowledge vs. ignorance

Loss and impact on others

Loss of innocence

Love at first sight is real

Love comes at a price

Love conquers all

Materialism leads to downfall

Persecution vs. mercy

Perseverance, or the will to
    survive

Power vs. wealth

Pride comes before the fall

Projection of true self

Quest for power comes with
    consequences

Secrecy vs. trust

Self-preservation vs. self-
    sacrifice

Self-reliance vs. trust

Skill vs. strength

Standing up for what's right is
    the greatest reward

Survival of the fittest

True friends are like gold

True love endures

Trust in karma, or that life
    will all work out

Trust those close to you

Trust your instincts

Wisdom comes with
    experience

Acknowledgments

After almost a decade in this industry, I consider myself fortunate for all the talented writers, editors, publishers, sales teams, and graphic designers I have met, whether online or in person. In some way, almost everyone I have encountered since launching my writing career has had an influence on this book. I have kept my ears open about the story ideas that resonate most with each subset of publishing and with differing personalities. This would be too many people to name, but if you and I have had a conversation about stories or ideas or books or publishing in the last several years, THANK YOU. You have helped shape this book.

As always, thank you to my husband and son (and to the Vancouver film industry) who have all afforded me the time and space to be able to write this book.

Enormous thanks to the entire team at New World Library for their dedication in packaging my nonfiction books so beautifully and for being so fantastic to work with. Jason, Monique, Munro, Kim, Jeff, and the rest of the New World Library team: It has been my pleasure to work with all of you.

Endnotes

1. Seek

Page 5, *Robert Frost tells us, "If you remember only..."*: Robert Frost in
Jack Foster, *How to Get Ideas* (San Francisco: Berrett-Koehler Publishers, 2007), 6.

Page 6, *Dr. Linus Pauling tells us, "If you want to have good ideas..."*:
Linus Pauling in Francis Crick, "The Impact of Linus Pauling on
Molecular Biology," The Pauling Symposium, 1996, Special Collec-
tions, Oregon State University, http://oregonstate.edu/dept/Special
_Collections/subpages/ahp/1995symposium/crick.html.

2. Passion

Page 14, *In her motivational book* Get It Done: Sam Bennett, *Get It Done*
(Novato, CA: New World Library, 2014), 60.

Page 15, *I like to use a fun and short online personality quiz from the
Smalley Institute*: For a free copy of the Smalley Institute personality
quiz, visit http://smalley.cc/images/Personality-Test.pdf. Some other
online personality quizzes include the NERIS Type Explorer personality test (https://www.16personalities.com/free-personality-test);
the EQ Test (https://www.arealme.com/eq/en); and just for fun,
J. K. Rowling's Pottermore Hogwarts House sorting (https://www
.pottermore.com/news/sorting-returns-to-pottermore).

3. Allies

Page 23, *In the book* Quiet: The Power of Introverts: Susan Cain, *Quiet: The Power of Introverts in a World that Can't Stop Talking* (New York: Broadway Books, 2013), 5.

5. Kinetic Energy

Page 32, The Brain that Changes Itself *by Norman Doidge explains*: Norman Doidge, *The Brain that Changes Itself* (New York: Penguin, 2007), 26, 42, 86.

Part II: Generating Sparks

Page 38, *For more on developing a story plan*: Denise Jaden, *Fast Fiction* (Novato, CA: New World Library, 2014). For a copy of the story plan, visit http://www.denisejaden.com/storyplan.html.

6. Observational Skills

Page 42, Your Artist's Brain *by Carl Purcell tells us*: Carl Purcell, *Your Artist's Brain* (Cincinnati: North Light Books, 2010), 12.

7. Fun and Games

Page 64, *Elin Kelsey tells a story of squirrels who learn how to cross*: Elin Kelsey, *Wild Ideas — Let Nature Inspire Your Thinking* (Toronto: Owlkids Books, 2015), 5.

Page 72, *In her online course on coming up with high-concept story ideas*: For more on Jessica Brody's online course, see https://www.udemy.com/writing-mastery-creating-high-concept-ideas-that-sell.

9. Following Through

Page 84, *When we think of "inventions," we think of Thomas Edison*: The inventions in this paragraph come from Robert Arp, *1001 Ideas That*

Changed the Way We Think (New York: Atria Books, 2013), 283, 316, 491.

Page 85, *Even a meme on Facebook, according to Robert Arp*: Arp, *1001 Ideas.*

Page 88, *Thomas Edison is quoted as saying, "I have not failed..."*: Edison in J. L. Elkhorne, "Edison: The Fabulous Drone" *73 Magazine* 46, no. 3 (March 1967), 52.

10. Troubleshooting Problems

Page 94, *In her book* Get It Done, *Sum Bennett asks this important question*: Bennett, *Get It Done*, 46.

13. Be Positive

Page 111, *In* The Happiness Project, *Gretchen Rubin suggests we shouldn't*: Gretchen Rubin, *The Happiness Project* (New York: Harper-Collins, 2009/2015), 183–85, 318. This idea is also shared on Rubin's blog: http://gretchenrubin.com/happiness_project/2012/07/a-paradox -of-happiness-spend-out-to-become-rich.

Page 114, *Great, you're more fortunate than the 758 million adults*: From Statistics on Literacy, from UNESCO Institute of Statistics, http://www.unesco.org/new/en/education/themes/education -building-blocks/literacy/resources/statistics.

14. Get Active

Page 118, *A 2013 report in the* Telegraph News *discussed how*: Sarah Knapton, "Lacking Inspiration? Exercise Found to Boost Creativity," *Telegraph News*, December 3, 2013, http://www.telegraph.co.uk /news/science/science-news/10491702/Lacking-inspiration-Exercise -found-to-boost-creativity.html.

Page 118, *"Physical activity gets your mind into the bodily experience..."*: Keith Sawyer in Sally Koslow, "How Exercise Makes You More Cre-ative," *Health*, September 3, 2001, http://www.health.com/health /article/0,,20412092,00.html.

Page 118, *In* The Creative Habit: Learn It and Use It for Life, *legendary choreographer*: Twyla Tharp, *The Creative Habit: Learn It and Use It for Life* (New York: Simon & Schuster, 2003), 18.

Page 119, *A 2005 report in* Creative Research Journal *suggests*: David M. Blanchette et al., "Aerobic Exercise and Creative Potential: Immediate and Residual Effects," *Creativity Research Journal* 17, nos. 2–3 (2005), 257–64.

15. Rest

Page 122, *And as Jack Foster tells us in his book*: Foster, *How to Get Ideas*, 19.

Appendix A: Names

Page 137, *For additional character names, including specific ethnicities*: For help brainstorming names, try these online resources. For names by ethnicity, try The Character Name Generator (http://character.namegeneratorfun.com), The Ultimate Random Name Generator (http://www.atlantagamer.org/iGM/RandomNames/index.php), and Behind the Name (http://www.behindthename.com/random), which includes Greek myth! For fantasy names, try the Fantasy Name Generator (https://www.fantasynamegen.com).

About the Author

Denise Jaden wrote her debut novel, *Losing Faith*, in twenty-one days during NaNoWriMo in 2007, and she loves talking with writers and students alike about drumming up story ideas and her just-get-to-the-end fast-drafting process. Her other young adult novels include *Never Enough*, *A Christmas Kerril*, *Foreign Exchange*, and *Avalanche*. Her nonfiction books for writers include *Writing with a Heavy Heart* and the NaNoWriMo-popular guide *Fast Fiction*. In her spare time, she homeschools her son (who is also a fast-drafter of fiction), acts in TV and movies, and dances with a Polynesian dance troupe. She lives just outside Vancouver, British Columbia, with her husband and son.

For regular inspiration and writing tips from Denise delivered right to your inbox, sign up at www.denisejaden.com/tips.